**Look Forward
Hopefully**
♥♥

To Amy,

May you always live

with Hope!

Bob

Look Forward Hopefully

Bob Mueller

Chicago Spectrum Press
Louisville, Kentucky

© 2002 by Robert J. Mueller

Chicago Spectrum Press
4824 Brownsboro Center Arcade
Louisville, KY 40207
1-800-594-5190

Printed in the U.S.A.

ISBN 1-58374-044-9

This book is for Kathy,
My wife and soul mate.
In her love, I have experienced the promise
Of what I always believed was possible
Between a man and a woman.

CONTENTS

ACKNOWLEDGMENTS

Everyone needs a cheering squad rooting them on, and my cheerleaders are sensational! They include:

Dorothy Kavka, my editor and publisher, who for years has been encouraging me to put my monthly columns into a book.

Kay Johnson and Carolyn Martin who spent many hours reading and making many helpful suggestions.

Stephanie Smith and Marilyn Ferguson, hospice co-workers, for their assistance with proofreading, marketing, advertising and promotion.

Kathy Mueller who gave countless hours typesetting, editing, proofreading and adding her touches to make each chapter more readable. She is a being of light whose belief in and appreciation of my work fills my heart and makes me soar.

Thanks to the many people who have called or sent letters over the years encouraging me to publish: Cathy Zion and Anita Oldham of *Today's Woman* magazine, Rob Patterson, my Rotarian and Hospice and Palliative Care of Louisville colleagues, and numerous others. Your encouragement has made this book possible.

INTRODUCTION

For fifteen years I was a minister in four large Roman Catholic parishes. In addition, I have spoken in many places for non-profit groups dealing with hospice, literacy, and dyslexia. I cannot count the people I have talked to over the years; I have a lot of mileage on my mouth.

It is my deepest feeling that the major problem of people is that they do not have a high enough opinion of themselves. They feel guilt and shame, and unworthiness and inadequacy. Feeling these emotions, many people run from life and never live up to their best. If we do not have the right opinion of ourselves then we will not properly love others. Throughout these pages I keep saying, "Love yourself, recover your sense of wonder, and look forward hopefully."

The date of September 11, 2001 marks a tragic episode in world history that we will never forget. When we are troubled, we must remember our need for each other. At a funeral service for a lovely mother, I was deeply impressed as the four children stayed so close to their father and to each other. At this time of great sorrow there was a real need. In times of illness it means a lot to know that somebody cares. In fact, in our latter years, having the realization that somebody loves you is one of the most stimulating experiences of life.

Two songs that have been around a long time are "Just Walking in the Rain" and "Singing in the Rain." The two go together: when the rain comes into your life and everything seems dark and dreary, keep walking – don't stop. And as you walk, you will begin to sing. We can't prevent the rain from coming, but through faith in our inner resources and with our Higher Power working in us and for us, we can learn to sing in the rain. When you are hurt, the temptation is to complain. But when your heart is trusting in your Higher Power, the resulting song in your heart will dry your tears.

Sarah Williams wrote a poem called, "The Old Astronomer." In that poem are these lines that have comforted me in light of September 11th:

"Though my soul may set in darkness
It will rise in perfect light,
I have loved the stars too fondly
To be fearful of the night."

Through the years I have kept a file of quotations, poems, and inspirational material. Sometimes I do not have the proper source for some of this material. It is my intention always to give credit, but when I do not give proper credit it is because I do not know where to give it. I am certainly grateful to many people whose writings have inspired me especially Charles L. Allen, Dr. Wayne Dyer, Matthew Fox, Joseph Gallagher, Hermann Hesse, Abraham Lincoln, Anthony de Mello, Thomas Merton, and Wayne Muller.

The messages in this book are, for the most part, my columns that have appeared in *Today's Woman, Reporters,* and *Karefree Times,* which in turn, came out of my sermons in parishes in Louisville and Elizabethtown, Kentucky, where I have served.

PART ONE - IDENTITY

The Basic Facts About You

Some time ago a man was talking to me about the problems in his life. Finally, he made this statement, "The main trouble with me is I'm a phony."

My reply to him was that in some degree, in some area of life, every person is a "phony." The simplest definition of a "phony" is "a person who seeks to appear to be something that he or she is not." I notice that most of us enjoy being described as something more than we really are.

You will never offend a ten-year old boy by saying to him, "You look old enough to be fourteen." When a mother and daughter are shopping together in a store, for the clerk to say to the daughter, "Would your sister also like to buy a dress?" never offends the mother!

In the hospital, a medical student is not offended by being called "Doctor." If you are stopped for speeding, you never make a mistake by calling the police officer "Captain." Door-to-door salesmen have been known to say to the woman who answers the door, "Is your mother in?"

The truth is, there is a touch of phoniness in all of us. On the other hand, one of the greatest inspirations in life is the person we can be constantly calling to the person that we are. Marvelous things can happen to us. The greatest freedom we can attain is the freedom which frees us to become our true selves.

Whether we see any phoniness in ourselves or not, there are three basic facts about "you," whoever you are.

First, you are. There are billions of people on this earth. You are one of them and you are different from any of them. **Second, you are becoming.** You are either becoming more or you are becoming less. You are becoming better or you are becoming worse. You are moving toward strength or you are moving toward weakness. You are growing in fellowship with others or you are becoming more and more wrapped up within yourself. You are moving toward life or you are moving toward death. No one of us is standing still. **Third, you have the choice of only one road and that is the road that begins right where you are.** The only starting point for you is the person you are right now. You can't go back one day, one year, or ten years. Life moves in only one direction. You can become free to be you.

For many summers a composer named Giocchino Rossini would go out to some small village in Italy, one which could not afford an opera, and he would write an opera which the people of that village could perform. One summer, he auditioned all of the talent in this small village and the only woman who could possibly be a leading lady was limited to one good note. It was a middle B-flat. Rossini was not discouraged; he went right ahead and wrote the opera in which the leading lady had only the one note to sing. But he surrounded that middle B-flat with such beautiful harmony that when she sang her one note, it was like the sound of an angel from heaven.

This is what life calls us to do. We each must sing the notes we can sing. Then life surrounds us in such a way that the effort we make is beautiful, it is useful, and it is satisfying.

Believe in Yourself

Do you believe in yourself? If your answer is negative, you have a serious handicap to overcome. I assure you, however, you can learn to believe in yourself if you will take three essential steps.

The first one is to **formulate a mental picture of yourself succeeding.** There is an old story of an outcast beggar who was sitting across the street from an artist's studio. The artist saw him and quickly began to paint his portrait. When it was finished, he called the beggar over to look at it. At first the beggar did not recognize himself.. "Who is it?" he kept asking. The artist smiled and said nothing.

The beggar kept looking at the portrait until recognition began to dawn. Hesitantly he asked, "Is it me? Can it be me?" The artist replied, "That is the man I see in you." Then the beggar made a wonderful reply, "If that's the man you see," he said, "that's the man I'll be."

Sooner or later, all of us become the person we see ourselves to be. If you develop creative faith in yourself, eventually your faith will recreate you. If your mind is obsessed by thoughts of insecurity and inadequacy, it is because you have allowed such thoughts to dominate your thinking over a period of time. The only way to overcome those thoughts is by putting into your mind a positive pattern of ideas.

When you plant in your mind a mental picture of yourself succeeding, your mind will at first resist that picture. It takes much less mental effort to picture failure and our minds, like running water, seek the easiest course.

Your mind will seek to block your picture of success by building up obstacles. But over and against these obstacles, think of your assets and you will see that you have more for yourself than against yourself. As you tenaciously hold to your mental picture of success, eventually your mind will accept it and gradually all your powers will focus on that picture and begin to complete it.

The second step to believing in yourself is, **be willing to be yourself**. One of the quickest ways to depreciate yourself is to become awestruck by other people and to attempt to copy them. You can be you better than you can be anybody else. In fact, you are the only person you can be. When you try to be somebody else, you end up frustrated and defeated.

Michelangelo once bought an inferior piece of marble, which no one else would buy. Asked why he bought it he said, "Because there's an angel in there and I must set it free." Then he went to work with hammer and chisel and carved a magnificent statue of an angel.

That story reminds us of the fact that within each of us there is a finer person waiting to be set free. You do not need to be someone else. You have the person within you if you will only let it come out. As you develop your finest self, you develop marvelous self-confidence.

Consider the third step for it is the most important of the three. **Get into a right relationship with your higher power**. Within us are certain spiritual mechanisms. When we use them rightly, we have the ability to accomplish things far beyond our normal capabilities. Believe in God and you will believe in yourself.

William James had a deep understanding of human nature. He said, "Every sort of energy and endurance, of courage and capacity for handling life's evils is set free in those who have a deep spirituality." Note, what he is saying – you have energy, endurance, courage, and capacity, but spirituality is the key that unlocks these powers within you and sets them to work.

The Person You Can Be

In his very first political speech, Abraham Lincoln said to the voters of Sagamon County, "I have no other ambition so great as that of being truly esteemed by my fellow men." Look into the hearts of most people and you will find their greatest desire is the same as was Lincoln's. Yet, many feel they have missed this goal.

Many with hungry hearts give way to self-pity, become emotional invalids, and spend the rest of their lives bitterly nursing themselves. But others refuse to give up, and instead do something positive and constructive to meet their need.

A high school girl was elected president of her class. Her father asked "How did that happen?" She replied, "It did not happen, I happened it."

Learning to become sure of one's self and learning to be the person you can be are very important lessons to be learned in the school of life. I have come to the conclusion that the four main obstacles to personal development and power are self-pity, false pride, a martyr complex, and a sense of inferiority.

1. **Self-Pity.** One of the easiest things in the world is to feel sorry for yourself. When one is disappointed or defeated, it is indeed simple to indulge in an overdose of self-sympathy. This will destroy your determination and rob you of your self-respect.

2. **False pride.** This is one of the great enemies of the soul. It keeps you from admitting to others that your attitudes and actions have been wrong and from confessing to yourself your own weaknesses and mistakes. Pride gives you a false sense of values and it closes the door to a better life.

3. **A martyr complex.** It is so easy to feel you are carrying burdens greater than anyone else has borne, to parade your sorrows and difficulties and develop a desire for sympathetic attention. Just as some people become addicted to liquor or other drugs, others become addicted to sympathy. Because some folks are afraid or unwilling to face life as it really is, they invent all sorts of misfortunes to gain attention. This is the reason so many people "enjoy" poor health.

4. **A sense of inferiority.** The basic cause of inferiority is a comparison of ourselves with others. When we are convinced we have a purpose in life, then no matter what any other person is or does, we find in our hearts a sense of personal satisfaction that eliminates envious comparisons.

My wife and I have developed the healthy habit of purging our home every six months of all items we no longer need or use. It's a way of living simply and creating greater spiritual abundance. Our unused items we give to the poor or sell in a yard sale. We continue to learn that to create abundance, we must let go of the obstacles and the unnecessary in our life.

We need a Lincoln today. We need the emphasis Lincoln placed on human values. Lincoln would forcibly remind us that what we are is far more important than what we have.

Recently someone sent me a book entitled, *How To Sell Yourself.* There are countless books and tapes of that type on the market. Books on how to develop our personality, how to succeed, etc., are best sellers today.

But Lincoln said it so much better and he did not need to write a book to say it. "Live a decent, clean life, work hard and trust God."

Lincoln gave us three fundamentals:

1. **A clean life.** There is no substitute for right living.
2. **Hard work.** A man once said to Thomas Edison, "You are a genius." He replied, "Before I was a genius, I was a slave." There are no easy effortless pathways to greatness.
3. **Trust in God.** It is recorded that night after night Lincoln fell on his face in the White House, dug in the carpet with his long bony fingers and agonized before God to save this nation.

He did not pray that God would be on his side. He prayed that he might be on God's side. He became the person you can be.

Growing Up

Life brings no greater blessing than a child, but it is a heart-breaking tragedy for a child to never develop physically or mentally. Some people never mature. Let me list several characteristics of little children:

1. Children become very upset over any personal hurt. If pins prick the flesh, they will cry as if deadly wounded. They are not the most concerned about the suffering of others. They weep mostly for themselves.
2. Children want to be the center of attention. They are jealous of all about them. They are willing to play if they can choose the game. They demand applause and appreciation.
3. Children have to be taught to be thankful. Gratitude for them does not come naturally. They take all blessings of life as a matter of course.
4. Children owe nobody anything. Their attitude is to get all they can but they have little obligation to any person. They rarely think of what they owe their parents or the society in which they live.
5. Children are completely self-centered. They live in a world that revolves around themselves.

When we grow up and put away childish things, it does not mean that tears never come to our eyes. It does mean that tears are reserved for causes that deserve them and are never given to petty trifles. A mature person can and does weep over personal hurts but more often the tears of love are for the hurts of others.

When we grow up, we still appreciate the approval of others, but we go on living and working and serving even when there is no recognition by others. Also, gratitude and appreciation of others is one of the flowers of mature love. Love is always glad to say, "Thank you." Love puts away childish things. It grows up.

One of the unexplainable but true mysteries of life is that you never lose what you give. Send out love and love comes back. Send out hate and hate comes back. Send out mercy and mercy comes back. What we give, we get.

Recently I flew over the Ohio River for about a hundred miles. It was a beautiful moonlit night and the great river below our plane looked like a flowing silver ribbon as the soft beams of the moon played on it. It gave me a tremendous thrill to watch the river, one of the greatest in the world. For centuries it has been giving all that it has to the even greater Mississippi which in turn gives its water to the Gulf of Mexico.

But suppose the Ohio decided it could not afford to give so freely, that instead it began to hold back water for fear it would run dry. Then it would cease to be a river and become a swamp. As a swamp it would be an ugly thing, No river and certainly no person every really begins to live until they find something big enough to give themselves to.

So often we get obsessed over whether or not we get the credit or the recognition. And then we miss the big picture. Our ambition takes over. Once a pen remarked, "I am writing a book." But the ink replied, "I am writing the book. You could not make a mark if it were not for me." The paper interjected. "But what could either of you do without me?" Then the dictionary said, "If I did not supply the words, no book could be written." And all during the argument the author just smiled.

One day when Toscanini was conducting a rehearsal at the Metropolitan Opera House, a soprano soloist, who was famous and temperamental, objected to the maestro's suggestions. "I am the star of this performance." she exclaimed. "Madame," Toscanini replied quietly, "in this performance there are no stars." In the performance of love, there are no stars.

The absence of love is the explanation of the unhappiness and restlessness of vast multitudes of people today. Love is the one quality of character - the only one – about which we can say, "If a person has this, his life is good. Without this, no matter what else a person may have or do, life is bad." What we give, we get.

Humility and Timidity

Through the years I have come to realize that I get humility and timidity mixed up. Humility is wonderfully good, timidity is defeating and bad. There is no virtue in being "a timid soul." The basis of timidity is that we take ourselves too seriously. We must quit thinking about ourselves all of the time and start thinking about someone else.

Timidity is nothing but a form of self-reference and egotism. When we quit thinking about ourselves and start thinking about something greater than ourselves, our characters are transformed and we become courageous instead of timid. If you are a shy, timid person, you relate everything to yourself. You are the center of your own thoughts.

Some years ago, a young artist asked me to come and conduct a special service of dedication for a studio she had opened. She told me a wonderful story about herself. When she was a young child, she was severely burned, and it left large and unsightly scars on her face and neck. She became very self-conscious about those scars. She felt the children at school made unkind remarks about her and she had almost no friendly contacts with other children. During the years, she had several operations to eliminate those scars. Later she went to art school but did not do very well. She believed that her teacher was not interested in her. She became disheartened and discouraged.

Then she told me that one day she read Ralph Waldo Emerson's statement, "Neither you nor the world knows what you can do until you have tried." The next day she went to school a different person. Emerson's quote kept running through her mind. She did more that day than she had been doing. At the close of the class period she was behind a little partition washing her paint brushes. The teacher did not know she was there, and she heard him say to someone else, "If that girl would only wake up, she could become a really great artist."

She told me that was the most thrilling thing she had ever heard. For the first time she felt somebody had expressed faith in her. The next morning she got to school earlier than she ever had before. She worked harder, she accomplished more, and she graduated high in her class. The day we dedicated her studio she said to me, "I have no hesitation in undertaking this studio; I know it will succeed."

Each one of us has something in our lives that is trying to defeat us — that robs us of our power — that makes us shrink back. We can surrender to these things and become another "timid soul." On the other hand, somewhere in life we can find the inspiration to get up and get going. There is such a thing as reaching a point at which we are not worried about whether or not we are defeated. The thing we are concerned about is the feeling that we have tried — and winning or losing is not the most important thing.

Isaac Newton captured humility well when he said, "I do not know what I may appear to the world, but to myself I seem to have been only a boy playing on the seashore, and diverting myself in now and then finding a smoother pebble or prettier shell than ordinary whilst the great ocean of truth lay all undiscovered before me."

A man who celebrated his fiftieth wedding anniversary also described humility well he told me, "A man is always as young as he feels, but seldom as important."

A certain French Marquis was raised to his grand and exalted state from very humble surroundings. He had been a shepherd in his earlier days and so, in his palace he had one room known as "the shepherd's room." In that room were reproductions of hills and valleys and running streams and rocks and sheepfolds. Here were the staff he had carried and the clothes he had worn as a lad when herding his sheep. When asked one day the meaning of this he replied, "If ever my heart is tempted to haughtiness and pride, I go into that room and remind myself of what I once was."

Love Yourself

It is my deep feeling that the major problem of people is that they do not have a high enough opinion of themselves. They feel guilt and shame and unworthiness and inadequacy. Feeling these emotions, many people run from life and never live up to their best. I think true love begins by loving ourselves. If we do not have the right opinion of ourselves, then we will not properly love either God or other people.

To many people the idea of loving themselves is a totally wrong concept, and certainly the thought of loving yourself, in the minds of many, is utterly ridiculous. Many people fix in their minds that living the highest life means being dead to themselves – giving themselves – forgetting themselves – losing their lives – suffering for a cause – and on and on. It has been said over and over, "God first, others second, me last." Within the right interpretation, all of these expressions are valid and most acceptable.

Never get the idea that loving yourself means excluding others. Genuine self-love is never egocentric or selfish. Loving yourself does not mean that you are seeking as much as possible out of life and willing to give as little as possible. Neither is self-love the same as pride, arrogance, a sense of superiority, or an exaggerated feeling of importance. True self-love is mirrored in our attitude toward God and others. We look at others through the attitudes that we have toward ourselves. "Learn to love yourself" is really a starting place.

Remembering some bad decision we say, "I could kick myself for being so stupid." We look back on actions in some yesterday with shame and remorse and deep guilt. We cannot forget – we refuse to forgive. Instead, we relive and rethink over and over some wrong we did until we think ourselves into despair and self-degradation.

There are many other reasons why people hate themselves, such as, discrimination they have received because of their race, color, national origin, sex, etc. We depreciate ourselves because we lack the talents someone else possesses. Some people do not have the education that they wanted and they need and they mourn over opportunities that are now gone.

Learn to love yourself in order to stop hating others. We transfer to others the attitude we have toward ourselves. Loving ourselves, we wish good for other people. Hating ourselves, we want others pulled down to our level. Not being happy with ourselves, we are not happy with anybody else.

When people are mean, it doesn't mean they hate us. It's more likely because they are miserable about something. Probably some other person has been mean to them, something they hoped for didn't come true, or they have done something they are ashamed to even contemplate.

The truth of the matter is, just for our own self-preservation, we need to learn to love ourselves. Hating ourselves:

- Distorts our personalities
- Blocks all happiness out of our lives
- Creates within us negative spirits
- Makes us cynical, complaining and contentious
- Ruins all of our relationships with God and others.

Notice that we are told to "learn to love ourselves." It is not something that comes with just a quick decision. You do not simply say, " I will start loving myself," and find it accomplished. If you wish to play the piano, it takes learning. If you wish to paint beautiful pictures, it takes learning. So it is with loving ourselves.

An eminent baby specialist had a standard treatment for frail newborn infants who failed to gain weight. When he came to the baby's chart during his rounds in the hospital, he invariably scrawled the following directions to the nurse in attendance, "This baby is to be loved every three hours."

PART TWO – OBSTACLES

The Giants We Face

David was not the last person to be confronted by a giant. In fact, we all have our giants and that is why so many people develop inferiority complexes. If there were no giants, you would not feel inferior.

Some of the giants in our lives are real. Others are imaginary. But whether they are real or not, the trouble comes when we allow the giants to make us afraid, when instead of giving our best, we give up and quit. Your giant may be some physical handicap, it may be a difficult job that is before you, and it may be a deep sorrow, a financial debt, a feeling of loneliness, a harmful habit, or one of many things. David did not minimize the strengths of the giant but neither did he let the giant minimize him.

Whenever I get discouraged, I like to think about some of the great names in history and the giants they faced. Sir Walter Scott limped through life on club feet. Napoleon was an epileptic. John Milton, who wrote *Paradise Lost*, was blind as was Homer, the great Greek poet.

Louisa May Alcott, who wrote *Little Women*, a book read by millions, was told by an editor that she had no writing ability and advised her to stick to her sewing. When Walt Disney submitted his first drawings for publication, the editor told him he had no talent. The teachers of Thomas A. Edison said he was too stupid to learn. F.W. Woolworth built a great chain of stores but when he was twenty-one years old he was not permitted to wait on customers in the store where he worked. His employer said he did not have sense enough to meet the public. Josiah Wedgwood whose name stands for lovely china, was a lame, uneducated, neglected boy.

Beethoven was deaf. Before Admiral Richard E. Byrd flew over the North Pole and South Pole, he was retired from the United States Navy as unfit for service.

William James spoke about "our first layer of fatigue." One may push and work to the point of exhaustion. Most people operate within the limits of this first fatigue. They never really accomplish much. He said that beyond this first level there is an inexhaustible power awaiting one who taps it.

Runners on a track team speak of catching their "second wind." Just as airplanes can break the "sound barrier," so people can break through the "fatigue barrier." Many people go through life doing only those things they are compelled to do. For them life is a hard experience and they are constantly tired. Others go beyond the call of duty and freely give themselves. They find life to be a stimulating, thrilling adventure.

All of life may be divided into two parts: the first mile of compulsion and the second mile of consecration. In the first mile, people are constantly demanding their rights. In the second mile, people are looking for opportunities. The mile of compulsion is a burden; the mile of consecration is a great joy.

Sometimes we are almost overwhelmed by the deep shadows which fall across our world and our lives. We become discouraged as we see the plagues of vice and crime, the horror of war, discrimination, the low state of morals, and all the other shadows. But let us remember that shadows are created by light and if there were no light, then there would be no shadows. The fact that we see shadows in our world is evidence of the existence of light, and thus the shadows become a source of encouragement and strength. The brighter the light, the deeper the potential shadows.

Several years ago I had the pleasure of talking with a man who repairs the windows in the Cathedral of Chartres in France. This man said the one color which has not disintegrated from the environmental elements during the centuries is the blue used by the ancient craftsmen. He declared that one reason Chartres is so stimulating to the human spirit is because of the deep blues through which the light filters.

If the color through which we look at the light influences our minds and spirit, how much greater are we influenced by the windows through which we look at life. Color your thinking with brightness and the giants you face will cease to dominate you.

Victims

Vast numbers of people are victims of the obstacle complex. These people have become convinced that certain difficulties or circumstances stand in their way and that it is impossible for them to reach the goals in life they most want.

This isn't an old story. It is as new as today's newspaper. We dream of being something better. We want a more abundant life. But we see obstacles in the way and we become shrinking cowards, saying, "I can't," "It's impossible," "It isn't for me." We hesitate, we stop, and we lose out.

Remember: success comes in "**can**", failure in "**can't**." So get hold of a **can**-opener and start using it.

Why do we fail to reach the top of our abilities in life? There are three reasons. First, we concentrate on the obstacles in our way instead of on our strengths. The fact is that every person has had obstacles to overcome. We say, "Others could overcome their obstacles, but my case is different." The only difference is that some people fight to overcome their obstacles, while others sit back and let their obstacles overcome them. Some people live on top of the world; others with the weight of the world on top of them.

A second reason why we fail to possess our individual promised land is that we are not willing to pay the price. Someone told me that he had to give up the hopes of a college education due to the lack of funds. I remember a boy who made his way through college by milking twenty-two cows every morning before breakfast and every afternoon after supper. Another got up every morning at three o'clock and worked four hours as a night watchman. I thought of many I know today who work all day and then go to school at night. These people were willing to pay the price.

Too many young people today, when they look for a job, are only concerned about two things: the number of hours and the amount of the salary. But the exceptional few forget hours and think opportunity.

Third, we miss our greatest levels because we don't use our faith. When you face a debilitating fear, handicaps, difficulties in your home life, an unpleasant job, or a stack of bills, remember that faith moves mountains.

Tonight before you retire, take your mind off your obstacles, and say to yourself, "I can do all things." Keep saying it over and over until you get the feel of it. Say it so many times that it begins to take possession of you. And as you possess faith and become possessed by faith, you will at the same time begin to possess your promised land.

When You Are Upset

Abbe Pierre has a phrase, "penicillin for despair." He declares that to be the world's greatest need. I am inclined to agree. Every person who has been plagued by anxious fear and upset feelings feels the need for "penicillin for despair."

I have had many people tell me that they go to bed and toss and turn for hours before sleep comes. Others have told how they would suddenly begin trembling, break into a cold sweat, feel constant fatigue, and an abnormal dryness in their mouth, a constant headache, or a palpitating heart. Some describe a deadness of feeling where they seemed to have lost the ability to love their own families, or even God. Some have shared inclinations to suicide.

For people who know the suffering brought by anxious fear, I have deep sympathy. I have had some of those same feelings. Nearly every normal person has at some time been greatly distressed, troubled, appalled, agitated or upset. Some people seem condemned to live with an anxiety neurosis as a constant companion.

In times of anxious strain we are reminded to "have faith" and all our troubles will magically disappear. This simply is not true. Some of the greatest saints have cried out for "penicillin for despair," even though they had deep faith.

We may be told our fears are imaginary. That is a grave misstatement. All fears are real. None are imaginary. It may be that imagination causes our fears, or it may be that we react with fear to some circumstances in life, but fear is not imaginary. We are told to "pull ourselves together," but we are not sure what that means. Many do not feel they have strength enough to pull even if they knew what to pull.

When we have a bodily infection, our physician gives us penicillin and soon the infection is healed. We know that anxious fears may come even though we have faith, and we should not feel ashamed because of symptoms generated by these experiences. But we must remember that there is "penicillin for despair." It isn't a pill or a shot in the arm. It is an action or a series of actions. In your moments of upset, do these three things.

1. **Find someone to listen to your heart.** There are times when it is good for us to be with crowds. There are other times when we need to be with trusted and close friends. It's wonderful to have someone to share our deepest thoughts. Often it helps to talk with a minister or a skilled counselor. It is also important to remember that when we are in a dark valley, our first impulse is to tell our troubles to every person who will listen. We want to tell our troubles because we need sympathy and we get satisfaction from the pity of others and from self-pity. We may deny this but it is true. However, be selective with your sharing.

2. **Look to your Higher Power.** Often this is hard to do because part of the mind wants to hold on to its worries and despair. That is the easy way out. To despair is to lose hope and to lose hope is to give up, to quit. Frequently we translate our despair into bodily illness. Maybe we don't become invalids but we never "feel well." Much sickness is merely an escape from reality. It is another easy way out, but it is never a solution. Deep down we are ashamed of our cowardice. We feel guilty for selling our courage to buy sympathy. When we look into the face of our Higher Power, we have hope because we know that all things are possible.

3. **Take positive action.** In the midst of despair, the temptation is to retire, to slip into illness, to surrender. It is a struggle to do something. Refuse to retreat into

yourself. Activity is often the best cure for the blues. Physicians tell us that our fears come from the higher brain centers while physical activity comes from the lower brain centers. When you begin to exercise those lower brain centers through physical activity, it lessens the tension on the upper brain. Operations are performed where specific parts of the brain are removed to decrease those thoughts of fear. I know many folks who say their daily exercise "straightens out my thoughts." A little poem by an unknown author expresses my thoughts about upset well:

Worry? Why worry? What can worry do?
It never keeps a trouble from overtaking you.
It gives you indigestion and sleepless hours at night
And fills with gloom the days, however fair and bright.

It puts a frown upon the face, and sharpness to the tone
We're unfit to live with others and unfit to live alone.
Worry? Why worry? What can worry do?
It never keeps a trouble from overtaking you.

Pray? Why pray? What can praying do?
Praying really changes things, arranges life anew.
It's good for your digestion, gives peaceful sleep at night.
And fills the grayest, gloomiest day with rays of glowing light.

It puts a smile upon your face,
The love note in your tone.
Makes you fit to live with others, and fit to live alone.
Pray? Why pray? What can praying do?
It brings God down from heaven,
To live and work with you.

When You Get the Blues

Why do I get blue and discouraged? Why do I get upset inside? Why am I so frustrated? We have asked these questions many times.

Periods when we are "blue" are part of the natural rhythm of life. I believe that the law of the tides is a basic pattern of all life. The tides rise and fall. The tides go out and they come back. We have moments of exhilaration and times of depression. There is an upbeat and a downbeat in the moods of human beings. No person lives on a perfectly even keel. In the words of an old spiritual, "Sometimes I'm up, sometimes I'm down."

A man once told me about a chart that determines the hours of the day when fish are active and will bite better. It is published on the sports pages and is called the "So lunar Fishing Guide." He told me it applies equally to humans. At certain hours we feel more active and we would be wise to plan our work day to take advantage of those times. I've been studying this guide and I believe there is something to it.

The problem is not these normal fluctuations of the human spirit; the problem occurs when we get into periods of depression and inner turmoil and can't rise up again. I recently read an interview with Cy Young, the great baseball pitcher. He won more games than any other pitcher who ever lived. In talking about it he said, "Back when I played, if a pitcher got into trouble on the mound, the manager didn't rush out to talk with us or send in a reliever. We just had to keep on pitching and pitch our way out of trouble." He went on to explain, "If I were off form, I'd keep on pitching until I got in form again." So it is in life. There are no relief pitchers to get us out of our jams. We just have to keep on pitching until we work ourselves out. We shouldn't just surrender to our moods.

A young pilot who flies jets in Florida told me that his greatest danger in pulling out of a dive is "blacking out." So it is in life. When our spirits are diving downward, it is easy to "black out" instead of "pull out." But you will never black out if you emphasize these three things:

1. **Never forget that you are important.** No person is useless. Maybe you have not found the place in life that you most want, maybe your life isn't big enough. No one else can duplicate you. Because of who you are and what you are, you can afford to believe in yourself and depend on yourself. You will learn to balance on your own two feet and develop a stimulating independence.

2. **Remember that you are needed.** This is true especially when you are discouraged and think all is lost. There is important work to be done that will not be done unless you do it. We all give ourselves to something. Many people give themselves to something that is beneath them. In times of depression, think bigger thoughts about what your life can amount to.

3. **Remember that there are several people in you.** You are a good person, but you also have a bad side. You shrink back from life, but you also face difficult situations with calmness and courage. You have the temptation to sink into a mud hole of life, but you also reach for the stars. Within you is one who is careless and doesn't care, another who is greedy and selfish, and another who is controlled by passions. But never forget, within you there is always a best self.

When factories first manufactured golf balls, they made the covers smooth. Then it was discovered that after a ball had been roughed up, the golfer could get more distance out of it. So companies manufactured them with dimpled covers. So it is with life. It takes some rough spots in your life to make you go farthest. The "blues" can change their hues.

When We Run Out of Gas

The other day my car suddenly stopped. I looked at the gauge on the dashboard and saw that I was out of gas. I might have called a mechanic and had him come and replace every worn part on the car, but still it would not have run. I might have had a new set of tires put on, but still I would have sat there. I might have washed and polished my car until it was as bright and shining as new. Still it would have gone no place.

My car had exhausted its power, and until a new supply of gasoline was put in the tank, the car would be dead and lifeless. We have marvelous power to use – oil and gas in the ground, electricity, atomic power all about us, and many powers yet to be discovered. Our progress has been determined by our ability to harness and use that power. If the sources of our power were suddenly cut off, all progress would come to a screeching halt.

Many times we "do not feel good," "are all run down," or "do not have any energy." People, like automobiles, can run out of gas. We can take vitamins and tonics, go on vacations, play golf, go fishing, look at television, read novels, and on and on, but the prophet long ago was right when he said, "There comes a time when only God in our lives gives us the power we need to keep going." It has been well said:

> We mutter and sputter,
> We fume and we spurt,
> We mumble and groan,
> Our feelings are hurt,
> We can't understand things,
> Our vision grows dim,
> But all that we need,
> Is a moment with Him.

We also need diversity in our lives to renew ourselves and to "have it all." I believe it's important to be friends with a variety of people to keep our tank full. As George MacDonald has said, "The love of our neighbor is the only door out of the dungeon of self."

Be a friend to someone significantly older than yourself. I have always found it valuable for someone older to be my mentor. As Charles Schulz of "Peanuts" fame stated, "If I were given the opportunity to present a gift to the next generation, it would be the ability for each individual to learn to laugh at himself." Choose someone older who can be your mentor. In that person you will find much distilled wisdom.

Find a friend who is much younger. Youthful Anne Frank once exclaimed, "How wonderful it is that no one need wait a single moment to start to improve the world." Youth have such enthusiasm and energy to inspire those of us who are older. They are filled with an appreciation for the wonder and mystery of life. A child can recharge your life.

Visit with someone who has been sick. There are two Latin proverbs that show the value of this particular friendship: "In time of sickness the soul collects itself anew" and "Sickness shows us what we are." I am always inspired with the stories of strength that our Hospice and Palliative Care of Louisville care providers share about those who are terminally ill. These care providers invariably claim that they receive more from their patients than their patients receive from them.

Love your enemy. It will drive them nuts. It will set you free. I love the humorous story about the magician who was sailing the Pacific, right after World War II, entertaining the passengers. With each amazing feat of magic, a parrot, who perched on his shoulder would squawk, "Faker, faker." No matter what the magician did, pulling rabbits out of hats, vanishing birds – cage and all, he would repeatedly cry, "Faker,

faker." The magician and parrot became bitter enemies. Finally the magician promised that he would do a trick that would out-Houdini Houdini. The night came, the wand was waved, the "woofle dust" was sprinkled. At that minute the ship hit a floating mine, which blew the ship to pieces. The next morning on a make-shift life raft the parrot was perched at one end, the magician at the other. Finally the parrot hopped over and said, "Okay, buddy, you win, but what did you do with the ship?"

Love animals, nature, and all creation. A monk once asked: "Is there anything more miraculous than the wonders of nature?" The Master answered: "Yes, your **awareness** of the wonders of nature." To be surprised, to wonder, is to begin to understand. Your well will never run dry and your tank will always be full.

What's Your Rush?

One day I walked along a road until I came to a cemetery. I remembered a prescription a physician gave to a patient: "Spend an hour a day for a week walking in the cemetery. Remember that the people here thought they had to do everything, but now the world is going along without them."

"Rushing" is one of the worst of our modern diseases. Watch the cars waiting for a red light. At the first flicker of the light changing, many drivers stomp down on the accelerator. If a car ahead hesitates for even a second, people behind it impatiently blow their horns.

I even notice signs of "rushing" at church. Some people sit on the edge of the pew and never really settle down. If the service runs a minute overtime, they begin fidgeting and looking at their watches. When the final blessing is announced, they rush toward the door. I sometimes want to stand at the door and ask, "What's your hurry?" Most could make no answer. They are really in no hurry; they are just afflicted with "rushing."

I spent an hour walking among the graves. During that hour I was the only person there. I thought about how quickly someone is forgotten and how others take our places. It is not as important that we carry the world on our shoulders, as we sometimes think.

Many times I have listened to the engines of a giant airliner. As the plane roars down the runway for take-off, it uses all its power to lift itself off the ground into the air. But very quickly after take-off you can tell that the pilot has eased back the throttle; the big plane climbs and finally levels off. Then the engines are throttled down still more. The pilot will tell you, "If I run the engines at full power for long, it will damage them." So it is with each of us. There are times when we must go at our own full power. But if we do not learn to ease back the throttle, level off, and hit a steady cruising speed, eventually we too will become damaged by the strain to our internal "engine". I'm not thinking so much of the strain we put on our bodies as that which we put on our minds.

I know a man who is confined to a wheel chair, yet he is burning himself out. His mind is constantly rushing. He worries about his business, he has an uneasy conscience which tortures him, and he is filled with unrest and tension. He has never learned to level off.

Why are people so rushed, so restless and ill at ease? Often it is because we have not found satisfaction in life. Maybe we are running away from a sense of failure. Several years ago a friend came to visit me. He had been drinking and could hardly walk up the steps. I asked, "Why do you drink the way you do?" He said, "I am trying to find a better world to live in." Not being able to face his world, he tried to escape into another world through alcohol.

We all have lofty ambitions which we struggle to reach. We want to get ahead, to excel, and to make a big contribution to the world. Yet there are conflicting desires in our hearts. We would like to have a little cabin out in the woods, smell the pines, and hear the soft rustle of the wind in the trees. It would be good to have a little stream running nearby and to listen to the gentle splashing of the water over the rocks. A log fire would be nice and a big rocking chair in which to rock slowly as we watch the red coals turn gray would be so cozy and comfortable.

For most of us, the cabin in the woods where we can get away from it all is not possible. But we can learn how to rest. If there is one lesson this generation needs to learn, it is how to take time to live. I talk privately with a lot of people, most of whom start the interview by saying, "I know you are in a hurry. . ." But long ago I learned you cannot counsel with people on the run. I tell many that they have already run past far more than they will ever catch up with.

Study some of the words of our language. The word "contentment" is derived from two Latin words: "con" and "tenio." It means "to hold together." We use an expression, "I went to pieces." That is an exact expression because it literally happens. I have been writing about inner tension. That is what we feel when, under some strain, we do not hold ourselves together and we develop within ourselves an inner war. We have tension today in the world. What is the reason? Two or more nations are at variance with each other. The world is not unified in its purposes and desires.

Notice the resemblances between the words "meditation" and "medication." If you will study them further, you will find that meditation is truly medication for one's body. Consider the words "wholeness" and "holiness." One means complete health, the other means completely without sin. The two go together.

Get quiet. Don't rush. Slow down. Meditate. See how it will deeply affect your own mind, body, and soul.

PART THREE – SELF CONTROL

Why We Worry

The word "worry" does not occur in the Bible, but often is in the minds of many people. Worry robs a life of its power and joy, makes many people sick, and even can destroy the desire to live. Sometimes we can conquer something if we know its cause, so I would like to list six causes of worry.

1. **We worry because we are hurt**. Sometimes we are hurt because of the loss of something. We lose our material possessions, our health, friends, jobs, or any number of things. More often we worry because we fear we may lose something.

Life hurts because of what it withholds. We dream, plan and struggle, but the prize eludes us. Hope is a wonderful thing, but continued unrealized hope has the power to break a heart. Many are hurt because of what happens to someone else. One whom we love is hurt; but, more often, we worry because of the success of someone else. Envy and jealousy have the power to hurt terribly.

2. **We worry because we refuse to accept life as it is**. I am not a fatalist, but there are some things in life that we cannot change and to refuse to accept that fact is a major cause of worry.

Someone wrote these lines about the weather: "After all, we are nothing but fools; when it's hot we want it cool; when it's cool we want it hot; we always want it the way it's not."

There are many things we cannot change. We must accept them as graciously as we can. It certainly does no good to worry about them.

3. **We worry because we refuse to accept our limitations.** I have heard people say, "I can do anything anybody else can do." This is a foolish and silly statement. You cannot do everything others can do, but you can do some things well and that is what counts for most in your life

4. **We worry because we are self-centered.** The best cure for worry is to go forth deliberately and lift the gloom off of somebody else.

5. **We worry because we are at war with our conscience.** We face decisions we dare not make, hear calls to duty we will not answer, and commit acts that violate our own ideals.

6. **We worry due to lack of faith.** Faith and worry cannot live in the same mind. Faith in yourself and faith in a higher power bring peace and strength.

One of the most common fears people face is the fear that something bad is going to happen tomorrow or some time in the future. An extreme example is a man who told me he was afraid he might die any day. I asked why he thought about dying and he said he was afraid that he had heart trouble. I suggested to him to see a physician. He had been examined and the doctor had told him his heart was in good condition, but he was still afraid. I asked why he was afraid of dying and he said he might go to hell. I suggested that he repent of his sins and get ready to die. He claimed he had done that, but was still afraid.

He told me that he worried because his wife might leave him. I asked if she had ever indicated in any way that she was thinking of leaving. He said no, but that he had known of other men's wives leaving them and he thought that his wife might leave him too.

Then he was afraid that he might lose his job. I asked if he was doing his work all right and if his employer had ever said everything about firing him. He told me he was doing a good job and his boss had always seemed pleased with his work. Still, others had been fired and he might be too.

This is such an extreme example that it seems almost incredible. Yet there are many people suffering, with a fear of something dreadful happening. We allow the thought of some possible disaster to rob our lives of all the joy and beauty that is ours.

Control Your Emotions

To get ahead in life and to be happy, we must learn to control our emotions. There are four simple suggestions that will work wonders for all who perform them.

First, **Study Yourself** and determine your weak spots. Achilles had a vulnerable heel and nearly every person has some particular weakness that is upsetting. For example, I know people who can endure prolonged physical suffering but will go to pieces at the slightest criticism.

One of my characteristics is impatience. I have friends who can fish all day in one spot and have a perfectly terrific time whether they catch anything or not. I can't do that. I actually believe I was born in a hurry, so that when things go slowly I get irritated. I have recognized that weakness and have made a lot of progress.

One afternoon I was driving out of downtown on a major expressway right at rush hour. The traffic was heavy and slow, and I had to crawl along. I was beginning to get upset and then I caught myself. I thought about how long it would take me to drive from where I was to where I was headed if there were no traffic at all. I decided it should take about ten minutes. Then I looked at my watch and calculated how long I thought it would take in that heavy traffic. Then I just relaxed, turned on the radio and settled down. It took me exactly sixteen minutes to get my destination, just six minutes more. I decided that my time is not so valuable that it was worth being upset.

Study yourself. What are the things that irritate and upset you? In most instances they are simply not worth bothering with at all. So study to strengthen yourself where you are emotionally weak.

Second, **Study People.** The study of people is the most interesting study in the world; so, instead of letting people upset you, study them objectively. For example, suppose store clerks are rude to you. Instead of getting angry and making a fool of yourself, start asking yourself why the clerks are rude. Perhaps a previous customer upset them and they were taking it out on you. A member of their family may be sick and they're worried. Perhaps they have a toothache, or are struggling with a debt and don't know how to pay it. If you knew all the facts, you probably would feel sorry for them instead of being angry. Instead of letting people upset you, get interested in them and you will learn a lot and maintain your own self-control at the same time.

Third, **Study the price you pay for getting upset.** You may have to pay a doctor and a medical bill. You may even have to go to a hospital. A physician told me that over half of his patients were sick because of emotional disturbances. Your emotional uncontrolled may even destroy your home. Nothing in life is more precious than the love of wife or husband. But if you keep on "flying off the handle," saying things you do not mean, pouting and nagging and acting like a spoiled brat, that love can be killed. To lose the peace and joy of your home is a mighty high price to pay. You can't do your work as well when you lose your self-control. Thus you drive away customers or cheat yourself out of a promotion. You are forced to swallow the bitter pill of seeing others get ahead of you.

Finally, **Recognize the presence of your Higher Power.** If we fully realize that at all times and in all places that we are in the presence of our Higher Power, it will help us control our emotions.

Thornton Wilder said it well, "That's the advantage of having lived 65 years. You don't feel the need to be impatient any longer." The prophet Isaiah said, "In quietness and in confidence shall be your strength." (30:15)

Envy Not

Envy and jealousy can slip up on the best of people. Oscar Wilde told a story of how the devil was crossing the Libyan Desert when he met a number of his people tormenting a holy hermit. They tried to involve the hermit in sins of the flesh, tempting him in every way they knew, but to no avail. Steadfastly the sainted man shook off all of their suggestions. Finally, after watching their failure in disgust, the devil whispered to the tempters, "What you do is too crude. Permit me one moment." Then the devil whispered to the holy man, "Your brother has just been made Bishop of Alexandria," and a scowl of malignant jealousy at once crowded the serene face of the hermit. "That," said the devil to his imps, "is the sort of thing which I recommend."

A fisherman friend of mine from Baltimore told me that he never needs a top for his crab basket. If one of the crabs starts to climb up the side of the basket, the other crabs will reach up and pull it back down. Some people are a lot like crabs. Envy and jealously may cause us to pull our friends down from their successes.

A salesman once told me that there are three things you always want the customer to believe in order to sell a piece of merchandise.

1. That he is getting the product for a lot less than it's worth.
2. That all the people he looks up to in the world have one.
3. That his best friends are going to burn with envy because he has one.

Envy and jealously can never possibly be satisfied. There was a farmer who was miserable because he could not buy the land adjoining his, but he would have to have all the land in the world to really accomplish this goal. But love does satisfy because it is not thinking of itself. A person who owns nothing can love and can feel happy and have a sense of well-being.

Rudyard Kipling, the brilliant English poet, was speaking to a graduating class at McGill University. He advised the graduates not to care too much for money or power or fame. He said, "Someday you will meet a man who cares for none of these things. . . and then you will know how poor you are."

Perfection

How can we expect to be perfect? What about our imperfections and our past mistakes? There is a tendency for us to say, "Well, I have already failed here, and there is no need for me to consider the idea of perfection further."

There is a tendency for us to say. "Why should imperfect individuals concern themselves about impossible ideals?" At the beginning of the New Year, we make resolutions only to see them broken. Then as the years go by, we begin to give up the idea of resolutions altogether. We have set goals for ourselves, only to fall short in discouragement.

We look at the world about us and see how many of our ideals have failed. For example, we have dreamed of a world of peace and yet even now we see war throughout the globe. We think of so many conditions in our society against which people have fought through the centuries and yet evil is still here. We have been disappointed in some we trusted. The margin between the declarations and the demonstrations of both ourselves and others has become so wide we feel, "What's the use of these impossible ideals any longer?"

Whenever I see a baby, I think: "Here is a perfect human being. This little one has never said or thought or done anything that is wrong. It is absolutely perfect." But suppose that baby remained as it is? As time went on, that would be a great tragedy. The glory of a little baby is that it has a lifetime before it in which to grow and develop. We are never concerned with what we are; our greater concern is what we may become, and that is what our dreams are all about.

In one of his speeches, the late President John F. Kennedy repeated a question that had been asked of him: "Why do we try to go to the moon?" His answer was: "Because it is there." We are always unsatisfied people, always reaching for things well above us. It is as Browning said: "A man's reach should exceed his grasp, or what's a heaven for?"

We may never attain perfection, but there is such a thing as attaining a perfect desire to be perfect. One of the differences between a swine and a sheep is this: the hog falls in the mud hole, and wallows in it, and enjoys it; the sheep falls in the mud hole, but it is not happy there, and struggles to get out. We must constantly struggle to rise above the mud, the wrongs, and the imperfections of this life.

Someone asked me: "Are you going on to perfection?" The answer is: "I am earnestly striving after it." None of us will ever become perfect, but we can always keep trying, and that is what God expects. As was once written:

You will never be sorry
For doing your level best,
For your faith in humanity,
For being kind to the poor,
For asking pardon when in error,
For being generous with an enemy,
For sympathizing with the oppressed.

Kindness and Good Manners

Kindness is described as being love in action. In this connection, we like to think of the well known words of William Penn. He said, "I expect to pass through life but once. If therefore, there be any kindness I can show or any good thing I can do to any fellow-being, let me do it now, and not defer or neglect it as I shall not pass this way again." Or as Wordsworth put it in "Tintern Abbey":

> That best portion of a good man's life
> His little., nameless, unremembered acts
> Of kindness and of love

The success of people living together, in what we call society, is based in no small measure on such simple things as politeness, tact, and good manners. The words "gentleman" and "lady" denote qualities of actions and of character which is extremely desirable – yes, even essential for people in association with each other.

Such acts as opening a door, saying "please" or "thank you," writing a note of appreciation, observing good table manners, allowing someone to enter a door ahead of you, saying something nice about a person when you introduce him or her, not contradicting someone telling a story, saying how much you enjoyed being with someone, cleanliness of body and of speech – and the list could go on and on – these so-called little things do make a difference in people's lives. Someone has well said:

> Politeness is to do and say,
> The kindest thing in the kindest way.

A man was once impressed by the courtesy of the conductor toward the passengers on a train. After the crowd had thinned out, he spoke to the conductor about it. "Well," the conductor explained, "about five years ago I read in the paper about a man who was included in a will just because he was polite. 'What in the world?' I thought, 'It might happen to me.' So I started treating passengers like people. And it makes me feel so good now I don't care if I ever get a million dollars."

This illustrates one of the main advantages of all the attributes of love – not only does it make for happiness in others, it comes back to bless our own lives.

We have heard the phrase "mind your manners" since we were children. In most instances, people who are reading these words do that, especially when we are in public. Sometimes we forget, however, when we are in private. It is sad but true that often we are the rudest to the ones we love the most. We all know that we should be at our best in the circle of those whose love means the most to us.

Chances are you do not realize what about you is most offensive to your mate or to those you are closest to. I recently played this game with my wife. I asked her what habit or behavior pattern in my life was most disagreeable to her. I was sure I knew what her answer would be. I had two negative factors in my life I expected her to mention. Instead she named four! We turned the game around and played it the other way and she ended up surprised also.

This is probably due to the fact that we just really never know ourselves as others know us. Play the game. Find out what in your life is most disagreeable to your mate or closest friend. Then by all means use your head and know that common decency and good manners would dictate that you correct or neutralize that negative quality promptly and permanently.

It may be a simple little habit. But remember

    It's the little things we do
        And the minor words we say
    That make or break the beauty
        Of the average passing day.

PART FOUR – RESPONSIBILITY

Responsibility for Ourselves

Time and again we blame the problems of life upon circumstances, when all the time, it is not circumstances – it is us. We cannot control circumstances, but we can accept responsibility for ourselves.

It is not difficult to talk about what other people think, to comment on what other people do, to spend our lives looking at other people and making judgments. We can talk about what the government does and about public morality; we can talk about the great social issues and what ought to be done about them; we can talk about the economic problems. The truth is, it's easy to talk and think about what's going on in the world. We can get upset about what other people are doing.

One of the serious mistakes parents make is they are never willing to let their children assume responsibility for themselves. We have all known parents who sought to direct every thought, word, and deed of their children. I have been in homes and asked a child a question where their mother would interject and say, "Tell him . . .." If I had wanted to know what the mother thought, I would have asked her. Let children answer questions. Let children make decisions. There are parents who never know when to quit directing. Even when children get married, there are parents who try to direct the children's homes and how their grandchildren are reared. Many marriages have broken up because of interfering parents.

Each of us recognizes the necessity of some self-responsibility. It is not easy to achieve, however. Bobby Jones was a great golfer. He started playing golf when he was five years old, and by the time he was twelve, he was an accomplished golfer. However, it was said of him that he would never win the big tournaments because he would always beat himself. He was known for his temper. If he missed a shot, he would become very upset, and he would often throw his clubs. He entered the national amateur tournament at the age of fourteen, and at that time, he was a good enough golfer to win the tournament. Actually, it was seven years before he finally won it. Someone said of him, "He was fourteen years old when he mastered the game of golf; he was twenty-one before he mastered himself."

We can blame our parents, the circumstances of our lives, and many, many other things for our own weaknesses, failures, and insecurities. Eventually, we need to face the fact that we are our own worst enemies, and we need to turn those enemies into friends. We need to become our own friend – to learn to love ourselves – to believe we are "somebody."

As we begin to believe in ourselves, we begin to see opportunities in life, yet every opportunity involves a risk. If a baby wants to learn to walk, he or she has to take the risk of falling. A parent must be willing for the baby to take that risk. As we grow and mature in life, in school, in work, in love, and on and on, the risk is our choice and we must take responsibility for ourselves. We make decisions and go on. There are times when those decisions don't turn out the way we wish, but still we go on. We can't spend our lives regretting what happened yesterday. It is difficult to lose and start again without talking about our losses, but that is what it takes to really grow up as a complete person.

To me, Charles A. Lindbergh will always be a hero. I think the reason I have looked up to him is because he was willing to say, "I will get in that plane alone and take off and fly across the Atlantic." There was nobody with him to help him if he got into trouble. He took the responsibility. That is the kind of people who fly across the ocean of life.

A man told me he spent some time writing down all of his material assets and adding up their value to see what he was worth. For most of us, that would not be an arduous task, because most of us do not have a vast amount of material resources. The thought, however, leads me to another kind of checking on ourselves. What are our real resources? We can see, we can hear, we can think, we can walk, and we live in a world of opportunities. Let us ask ourselves the question, "What powers do I really possess and how will I be responsible with them?"

Making Adjustments

As we go along through life we find a need for adjustments which must be made but are often difficult. One of the most serious and most obvious is an adjustment for a physical handicap. One adjustment not so obvious relates to our personal limitations.

Through the years I have counseled many students who had the desire to be among those in the top of their class but simply did not have the intellectual capacity to make it. It is not easy to face the fact that mentally and emotionally we are not equal to our dreams.

There is another adjustment that must often be made. It is adjusting to defects in those we love. As I have counseled couples who are planning marriage, one of the things I emphasize is that each must accept the other. Marriage is not a reformatory. Many divorces come out of one person trying to make their partner something he or she cannot be. There are times when divorce seems to be the only answer but there are many marriages that could be saved, if one would learn to accept and adjust. Parents must learn this lesson in reference to children. It is a painful experience when we come to the point of realization that our little boy or girl is not the brightest and smartest in the entire world. It is even more painful, later in life, when we realize that one of our children has imperfections that disappoint us and even break our hearts. But we do not give up on our love. Sometimes we love "on account of" and other times we love "in spite of."

As we make adjustments in life, we need to remember that life forever remains open-ended. The last word has yet to be spoken. Handicaps can be overcome. Life can drive away the darkness. Prisons may be unlocked. The lost may be found. Meaningful existence may be discovered.

Sometimes we hear the laughter of a child, or a song on the radio, or a sudden thought enters our mind, or we see an article in a newspaper or magazine – trivial things happen that bring lasting changes in life. The truth is, adjustments have been made every day of our lives. We just did not recognize them as they came. The minor adjustments have been made day after day and when we come to that major adjustment, we have the faith to believe it, too, can be made.

As we move through life, we hear thrilling calls and see challenging opportunities. But we also experience disappointments, defeats, and sometimes life loses its meaning. Then, along the way, as we keep going, we see new paths to follow, new mountains to climb, new hopes to cling to.

Let us bring to mind the experience of Franklin D. Roosevelt. Here was a man who had everything – social position, wealth, charm, ability, success in life – he seemed to have it all. Then one day he was home at Campobello. In the wonderful play *Sunrise at Campobello* by Dore Schary, we hear Mr. Roosevelt speaking to his wife in these words:

> Eleanor, I must say this – once to someone. Those first few days at Campobello when this started, I had despair – deep, sick despair. It wasn't the pain – there was much more of that later on when they straightened the tendons in my legs. No, not the pain – it was the sense that perhaps I would never get up again. Like a crab lying on its back. I'd look down at my fingers, and exert every thought to get them to move. I'd send down orders to my legs and toes – they didn't obey . . . .I turned to my faith . . . for strength to endure. I feel I have to go through this fire for some reason. Eleanor,

it's a hard way to learn humility – but I've been learning by crawling. I know what it meant – you must learn to crawl before you walk.

We know what Franklin D. Roosevelt went on to achieve: The only man in history of the United States to be elected president four times. He never was to walk on those legs again. He had to make a tremendous adjustment, but paralyzed legs or not, he not only learned to move about, he learned to become the world's most powerful leader.

Of course, there are constant changes to be made as we go along, but those changes can be made and we can keep going along. We don't stop, we don't give up hope, and we adjust.

Take Charge

A psychologist visited a penitentiary and began asking prisoners, "Why are you here?" The answers were interesting, even though expected. There were lots of reasons: "I was framed." "They ganged up on me." "It was a case of mistaken identity. It was not me – it was someone else." The psychologist concluded that you cannot find a larger group of innocent people than in a prison!

We are not responsible for what somebody else believes or does. To become a responsible self defines what it really means to come of age. We grow when we reach the point at which we can give answers for ourselves. One important area for personal responsibility I would like to emphasize is the controlling of our tongues.

There is a legend which has been often repeated but it does not hurt us to read it again. The legend tells of one with a troubled conscience, who went to the village priest for advice. He had repeated some slander about a friend and later had found that his words were untrue. He asked the priest what he could do to make amends. The priest told the man: "If you want to make peace with your conscience, you must fill a bag with goose feathers and go to every door in the village and drop a feather on each porch."

The peasant took a bag, filled it with goose feathers and did as he was told. Then he went back to the priest and asked, "Is this all that I need to do?" "No, that is not all," was the answer. "There is one thing more: take your bag and gather up every feather."

The peasant left. After a long period he returned, saying, "I could not find all the feathers, for the wind had blown them away." The priest said, "So it is with gossip. Unkind words are so easily dropped but we can never take them back again."

Let that story stick in your mind, and whenever you are tempted to say an unkind word, remembering the feathers, you will hesitate. The truth is many of us talk when we ought to be quiet. Gossip never does any harm – until someone makes an issue out of it. Gossip is both nasty and sickly but it will die if it is left alone.

I have a story I have enjoyed for many years. I think one of the reasons I like the story so well is because I have enjoyed the humor of the three persons involved. According to the story, ventriloquist Edgar Bergen and comedians Jack Benny and George Burns went to a restaurant for dinner. When they finished, Mr. Benny said to the waiter, "I will take the check." The waiter handed Jack the check and he paid it. On the way out, George Burns said to Jack, "It sure was nice of you to ask for the check." Jack replied, "I did not ask for the check, and that is the last time I will ever have dinner with a ventriloquist."

The point of the story is that we should do our own talking and not let somebody else speak for us. Many years ago I memorized what is called "A Short Course in Human Relations." Here it is:

The **6** most important words:
I admit I made a mistake.
The **5** most important words:
You did a good job.
The **4** most important words:
What is your opinion?
The **3** most important words:
If you please.
The **2** most important words:
Thank you.
The **1** most important word:
We
The **least** important word:
I

It's a Brand New Ball Game

On a summer afternoon I was listening to a radio broadcast of a Cincinnati Reds – St. Louis Cardinals baseball game. I heard the announcer say, "It's a brand new ball game." That meant the score was tied. It's like starting all over again.

So it is in life. Many of us come to a place where "it's a brand new ball game." Some situation has developed that has changed the old ball game. We begin all over again. When a couple gets married, "It's a brand new ball game." Also, when they get a divorce or when one of them dies or even when they keep living together but stop loving each other, "It's a brand new ball game."

Sudden life-changing experiences happen. It's time to begin again. It's something new. In a baseball game, when the score is tied in the seventh inning, they do not go back to the first inning and start over. They keep on playing. So it is in life.

In a baseball game at the end of the fifth inning, the score might be seven to nothing in favor of one team. Then in the very next inning, the other team rallies and scores seven runs. Now the score is tied. It's a brand new ball game.

What should be done about it? The team that was ahead and then got tied doesn't sit in the dugout, mourning that they let the other team catch up with them. They go out on the field and keep on playing.

Another wonderful fact about baseball is that there is no time limit like most other sports. It is a game of endless possibilities. In theory, a baseball game could go on forever.

More than any people I know, people who are living alone need the discipline of living now – not yesterday and not tomorrow. As we give ourselves to the present moment, we find new strengths, new powers, and new confidences. It is a marvelous experience when daily living becomes really an end in itself. We are no longer haunted by past unhappiness. We are no longer afraid of future possibilities.

In Margaret Mitchell's novel *Gone With the Wind*, old Grandma Fontaine, talking of the bitter experiences of defeat in the war said: "The whole world can't lick us. But we can lick ourselves by longing for things we haven't got any more and by remembering too much."

Many people suddenly find themselves in a new and frightening situation. They are alone. There is a tendency to look back with regret, remorse, self-reproach, and bitterness. When we do, the result is usually self-defeat. It is natural for radical changes and severe losses to leave us with a feeling of hurt.

That wound in our lives need not be permanent though, if we take several steps. First, we need to recognize that we do have a wound. To ignore or cover up a deep hurt creates more trouble. We catch ourselves reminiscing about the comfortable home in which we used to live, the marriage that was a success, the bank account that was adequate, or a time of health and well-being. As we keep looking back, we keep picking at the wound and it gets worse and worse, harder to bear. There comes a time when we need to bind up the wound and let it begin to heal.

There is a story about a traveler who stopped in a small town. He said to one of the natives: "What is the place noted for?" The native replied, "Mister, this is the starting point for any place in the world. You can start here and go anywhere you want to."

That's true for all of us. Wherever we are is the starting place. It's a brand new ball game.

Pass the Ball

No person becomes a success without the support of others. When people forget this and begin to attribute success to their own efforts, they are on the road to failure.

In the closing second of a critical game, a young basketball player scored the three pointer that won the game and put his team in the state tournament. He became an instant hero, but fame affected his attitude. He began to think of himself as a one-person team.

One day the coach heard the young player reliving the moment of glory. For the benefit of a group of admirers, the boy explained how he had sized up the situation as the final seconds of the game ticked away, how he gauged the distance to the basket and coolly evaded the defense, and so on.

Determined to salvage a good player if he could, the coach interrupted this heroic narrative with a question that put the whole event back in proper perspective. "Who," he asked, "passed you the ball?"

All of us have our moments of success but behind every accomplishment – every winning basket – there is someone who "passed us the ball." To ignore this basic fact by refusing to give graceful credit to those who have helped us, is to invite a sudden and drastic reversal of our fortunes.

As an example, there are those athletes who have made the mistake of assuming they were of more importance as individual stars than as team players. Almost invariably, such individuals find themselves scoring fewer and fewer points in each successive game for the reason that "nobody is passing them the ball."

We must never neglect to give credit where credit is due – not arrogantly or patronizingly – but humbly and in simple gratitude. I love Thurgood Marshall's quote: "None of us has gotten where we are solely by pulling ourselves up by our own bootstraps. We got here because somebody . . . bent down and helped us."

A man was traveling on foot through the mountains in a heavy snowfall. The climb was long and difficult and the traveler began to wonder whether he had the endurance to make it through safely. Suddenly, he stumbled over the prostrate form of another wayfarer, a man who, apparently exhausted by the cold and the steepness of the ascent, had laid down beside the trail.

Forgetting his own weariness and discomfort, the first traveler hurried to aid the unfortunate stranger. When the stranger began to show signs of life, the traveler forced him to swallow some water and finally got him on his feet and walking again. It was then that the traveler realized that in working hard to save the stranger he had saved himself, for now he felt warm and strong again. Together the men were able to make their way to the safety of a mountaineer's cabin.

This story, which has its counterpart in many occurrences of day-to-day life, poses an important question: "Which of the two men benefited most from the episode?" The truth is the more we help others the more we will benefit – providing we act unselfishly.

When we fall prey to self-pity, we would be wise to remember that there are others whose hardships and needs are far greater than our own. In helping these unfortunates we will find, invariably, that we are also helping ourselves.

PART FIVE – COPING

Memories

Living in a city can be a discouraging experience because we are confronted with so many problems. There are sections where the housing is inadequate and the people are poor. There are streets where it is dangerous to walk because of crime. Many people in the city are sick. There are those who are friendless and lonely, others who are discouraged and frustrated. In a city there are murders, rapes, automobile wrecks, and fires. There is polluted air. Every day people are buried who are dear to someone's heart. There is deep sorrow in the hearts of many people in every city. At times one feels a sense of hopelessness.

During the year, I sometimes drive out to the city's airport and get on an airplane. As the plane gains altitude I look out the window and see the city stretched below. It is a beautiful sight, especially at night, when all the lights of the city are shining. From the airplane I get a much more satisfying view of the city than when making my way through the narrow streets. Even though there are problems in the city, from the heights one sees the beauty and majesty of the city and is inspired by it.

So it is with life. Living in the present, we are constantly confronted with the trials and troubles of life. But when we look back at life through memory, like seeing the city from an airplane, we see life as a whole. The hard places are not visible, the pain and suffering is quieted, and the entire panorama is beautiful and inspiring.

Memory and hope are very closely connected. We use the same faculties to look both backward and forward. If we look back and see the wonderful works of creation, we will be inspired to look into the future and believe there are blessings ahead. Let us not condemn ourselves because of the memory of something past. Suppose you had no memory? Remembrance of the past preserves our identity. Without that memory we would never know who we are. We know that we are persons who are living now, but we must have in our minds the past in order to know what the now means. The result of forgetting the past is an emptiness and a lack of life today.

As we think of our past mistakes, let us also remind ourselves that our strengths and our abilities and our future are rooted and grounded in our past. I read about a woman who had a calendar on her wall which had only one day for each page. At the close of each day she would tear off that page and throw it in the wastebasket. To her consternation she realized that her calendar was growing thinner each passing day. So she changed her practice and instead of throwing the page for each day into the wastebasket, she carefully filed it with its predecessors. Then as the calendar grew thinner, the file of days she had lived grew thicker. So it is with life. Yes, we can look back with regrets and with guilt, but if you merely throw away the past, life for you gets thinner and thinner.

A minister friend of mine offered comfort to a mother whose child had recently died. This is what he said, "As burdensome as the grief of loss most certainly is, there is yet one grief heavier to be born, and that's the grief of never having possessed."

So we have possessed past days and past years. Maybe we did make some mistakes, though we also won some victories. We ask forgiveness for the mistakes and we are thankful for the good things. Because of the gift of memory, we are not impoverished because of what we have lost. We have **never** lost it.

A lot of people enjoy talking about the so-called "good old days," when there was less crime, fewer problems, and fewer worries. Enjoy memory as one of the greatest blessings of humankind.

Share the Grief

Often I have asked myself the question, "Why couldn't I help that person?" One answer is that there are some situations that nobody can help. Some time ago I visited with a father whose teenage son had just an hour before been killed in an accident. A friend was there with him, but the friend felt great despair. He said to me, "I have prayed with him; I have read him the Bible; I have tried to talk to him, but nothing helps. He will not respond to me in any way." I sat down with the father and simply said, "I do not see how you can stand to bear what has happened." It was the opening the boy's father needed.

Once there was a little child who went on an errand for her mother. She was late coming back and her mother asked for an explanation. The child explained that a playmate of hers down the street had fallen down and broken her doll and that she had helped her. The mother wondered what she could do to help mend the broken doll. The little girl made a marvelous reply, "I just sat down and helped her cry." There are times when we cannot solve other people's problems; we can only become a part of their grief.

I like the story of a missionary translator who was working with a tribe in the mountains of Mexico. He was struggling to get the right word for "comfort." One day his helper asked for a week's leave, and explained that his uncle had died and he wanted some days off to visit his bereaved aunt "to help her heart around the corner." That was just the expression the missionary needed.

As they walk through grief many people learn to make their own decisions, to forget their old selves, and to begin being better and stronger persons. They realize the need to keep on living and loving. There is marvelous power in accepting the fact that a change in our lives has occurred.

Something has been lost, but new experiences can be found. The valley of the shadow of death is never a place to live; it is a place to go through.

One comic-strip character uses the expression, "good grief," and truly grief can be good. Certainly there is life after grief, but many times there are changes. Yet frequently a sweet song comes out of grief. There is a legend about a bird in Australia called the thorn bird. The legend is that from the moment many of these birds leave the nest they go out in search of thorn trees and do not stop until the trees are found. Then they fly into the tree and pierce themselves upon the thorns. As the birds die they sing out a song that is considered more beautiful than even that of the nightingale. Out of their agony comes their greatest song.

I have known people who are like the thorn bird. They did not seek to be wounded on some thorn, yet being wounded, out of their agony came their sweetest songs. Over and over I have dealt with other's intense grief, and failed to help. I have watched people over a prolonged period, when their grief was devastating and self-destructive, hoping against hope, that somehow a break would come. There have been many times when the best help I could offer was not enough.

Long ago I learned that there are situations that I just cannot handle and am compelled to accept. I heard about a man who went to a marriage counselor about his wife. He explained that she was a terrible housekeeper and he just could not stand to live in a house that was constantly in utter disorder. He had begged, pleaded, complained, and done everything he knew to get his wife to keep the house better, but nothing helped. As he talked with the marriage counselor he was very fair to point out his wife's good qualities. Among other things, she was beautiful, intelligent, and a very loving wife and mother. He could not understand why she wouldn't keep the house better. Finally, the counselor said, "Let's face it – you are married to a beautiful, intelligent, loving, lousy housekeeper!"

In the business of helping people, let's you and I face the fact that there are some people that just are not going to be helped. They need to be accepted as they are. This is true too of people in grief. Sometimes the best we can do is accept them where they are.

It Really Is a Good World!

It was the beginning of a hectic weekend. The supermarket was jammed. The lines were long, and the girl's voice was already tired and bored as she mechanically told me, "Thank you. Have a good day." "Good day?" I thought cynically, remembering all the chores waiting for me when I got home. "Not a chance in the world."

Halfway home, I was forced to come to a complete stop by a parade. Crossing the road in front of me was a stately Canadian goose. She was unhurriedly leading a string of seven fluttering yellow-and-black goslings, who were scurrying in shifting disorder behind her. Bringing up the rear, in guard position, was another goose, the father I assumed.

By the time they reached the bank to my right, there was a line of cars behind me. Another line of cars had formed in the opposite direction. Mother and babies proceeded into the field to forage, but father goose turned at the top of the bank and as the cars slowly began to roll again, he opened his beak and hissed fiercely at us. The gander displayed such sheer bravado that was so unexpectedly outrageous that I laughed aloud. As I passed the other drivers, I saw that everyone else was also smiling and laughing.

No horns had honked and no tempers had flared. Pausing without impatience in the hustle and bustle of our clock-oriented schedules, we had all been friends for those few moments. We shared a chuckle at a simple spectacle – a family of geese crossing the road from a pond to a cornfield. As I drove home, my mood changed. It was now light and joyful. For some reason, it suddenly had become a good day.

We are misled by the news media today, which makes us feel that the world is filled with crime, corruption and evil, because such items make up the bulk of the daily news when they represent only a small segment of the people of the world. It's so important that we reflect on the good things of life.

Many people are not interested in knowing that possibly 100,000,000 people in the United States participate in some form of religious services every weekend counting TV and radio; that the poor are being clothed, sheltered and fed; that scholarships and tuition are being given to the worthy and diligent young students; that the sick are nursed back to health; that families are discovering the joys of reading and values; and that the world is filled with good people and good deeds. This should all be written in bronze so that thousands of years from now those who would unearth the plaque would know that the world in our time was also a good world.

Scoffers and cynics have lived in all times. People who trust look up. They enjoy nature and a gaggle of geese crossing the street allowing them to laugh and reflect. They know the blackouts, but they see the stars, too. Their duties in life are met with courage, because they know that an honest heart will find its fulfillment.

I used to love to visit an old music teacher who had a homely wisdom that refreshed me. One morning I walked in and said, "Well, what's the good news today?" Putting down her violin, she stepped over to a tuning fork suspended from a cord and struck it. "There is the good news for today," she said. "That, my friend, is the musical note 'A.' It was 'A' all day yesterday, will be 'A' next week and for a thousand years."

PART SIX – ENTHUSIASM

Enthusiasm

What a joy it is to meet people who are bubbling over with enthusiasm! The spirit of such people is infectious and they become inspirations to everyone around them. If they are in an executive or management position, the office or shop they supervise is a place where people enjoy their work and where achievement runs high. It's a fact that achieving success without being swept along by enthusiasm is next to impossible.

There is a story about a man who had fallen into a habit of complaining about the ordinary circumstances of his life and particularly about his job. He had lost his enthusiasm and he was too busy feeling sorry for himself to see the direct relationship between enthusiasm and success.

One morning instead of responding to the alarm clock, he turned over and went back to sleep for another 40 winks and he had a curious dream. He dreamed that he was struggling to get ready to go to the office but that nothing was going right. He tried to take a shower, but there was no water. He tried to shave, but there was no electric current. This meant of course, that he had to do without his morning cup of coffee and even without his breakfast. There were no newspapers at the newsstand and the poor fellow made his way to the bus stop only to wait 45 minutes with no bus in sight. Finally, in desperation, he turned to a passerby and demanded, "What's going on around here?" "Haven't you heard?" responded the stranger. "Everybody's inherited a million dollars! Nobody's working any more."

At that time the dreamer awoke. And suddenly the prospect of going to work looked better to him than it had in months. His morning shower felt great. His shave was sheer luxury. He savored the wake-up freshness of his coffee and the morning air smelled good as he hurried to catch his bus

What a difference enthusiasm can make in our daily lives. But it doesn't some easily. As we pass through life, we find that we must cultivate it through deliberate effort. How? One excellent way is through motivational reading and by attending lectures and seminars about a positive approach to life. I know many successful and enthusiastic people who wouldn't think of starting the day without meditation. They set aside twenty minutes every morning to reflect upon everything that is good in their lives, including the immediate challenge that needs to be met in a positive spirit of enthusiasm.

Every human being wants happiness, but very few find it because they do not know where to look. The poet Lowell wrote "We have a little room on the third floor with white curtains trimmed with evergreen and we are as happy as two mortals can be."

There is often more happiness in a cottage than in a castle. If it were true that the secret to happiness is riches, then millionaires would be the happiest people on earth, and we are sure that this is not true. Do you remember the story of the king who ordered that he be brought the shirt of the happiest man in his kingdom? They found the man. But he didn't have a shirt.

Enthusiasm and happiness aren't far off somewhere in the land of tomorrow. They don't depend upon a large bank account or a big automobile. We can find them right where we are today by looking for them in simple things, by greeting life as an adventure, by holding thoughts of love, cheer, and goodwill. Think of the happiness there is in good books, a quiet talk, a baby's smile, soft music, clean white sheets, a brisk walk in the fresh air, and the joy of loving and being loved.

Enthusiasm Reaches Goals

The famous football coach, Bob Zuppke, years ago once asked the question: "What makes a man fight?" He answered his own question by saying: "Two forces are at war in every fighter, the ego and the goal. An overdose of self-love, coddling the ego, makes bums of men who ought to be champions. Forgetfulness of self, complete absorption in the goal, often makes champions out of bums."

Bob Zuppke talked about a football player as he sees a high punt sailing toward him. The player knows that if he catches that ball, some two hundred plus pounds of bone and muscle of an opposing player will hit him and hit him hard. He knows he may be hurt. But he does not think of being hit or of being hurt. All he thinks of is the goal line that must be crossed.

A goal that has to be crossed gives power and stamina to life. Admiral Robert Peary wrote: "The determination to reach the pole had become so much a part of my being that, strange as it may seem, I long ago ceased to think of myself save as an instrument for the attainment of that end."

The world laughed at the idea of a flying machine. But the Wright brothers did fly. An old man watched them work and listened to them talking. He said of them, "I know as soon as I saw those boys that they were different from the folks down here. They had an idea. It possessed them. I used to listen as they argued by the hour. I didn't understand what they were driving at, but I understood them. I knew they would get there."

Pour out your own love and it comes back to you in the form of power and strength. A middle-aged man lay dying and he became mentally adjusted to it. In fact death seemed to him as a sweet relief from the heavy burdens of his life. He told himself that others would carry on his business. A few close friends would miss him, but they would soon become adjusted to his death. Then he thought of his wife. He thought of how she loved him and how he loved her, of how they had worked and lived together. His death would break her heart. Suddenly he began saying, "I cannot do this to her. I must live for her sake." And live he did. Under the power of a love that would not let him go, new life became his.

A woman did not have the money to go to school, but she did go! She carried a full course load, met her classes, and kept up with her studying. To pay her way, she worked as a security guard at night. She had only five hours a day to sleep. She ate only one hot meal a day, and she washed dishes in the cafeteria to pay for it. For breakfast she would eat a bowl of cereal in her room. She skipped the other meal.

A person cannot live on only one good meal a day and five hours' sleep. But she did it for an entire year. Not only that, she thrived on it. How did she do it? She fixed her mind on a great goal. She concentrated on the goal and that sustained her.

When one finds himself or herself being whipped by life, losing power and enthusiasm, the time has come to fix new goals – goals to which one can completely give oneself. What is your goal?

Recently I had cause to look up in the dictionary the word "enthusiasm." My dictionary defined it as "keen, animated interest in and preoccupation with something." It didn't say what the "something" has to be. It can be one of many things but we have all observed that until we find something to get excited about, we never really get very far. Enthusiasm will do six things for us:

1. **Enthusiasm brings out possibilities we are not using**. All of us have seen an athletic team

get excited and play "over their heads." The truth is they are not playing over their heads; what they have been doing is playing under their possibilities.

2. **Enthusiasm will make us work.** No two people have the same talent. Some people can sing, some people have business acumen, some people have athletic abilities, and on and on. We see people every day who can do things that we cannot do. The important thing is getting excited about what we can do. I like the story of the little boy in school. The class was studying the multiplication table and the teacher asked one boy to recite the nines. He was stumbling along, not doing too well. Finally he said, "Teacher, I do not know the nines very well, but I am a hound dog on the sevens." Now that kind of enthusiasm appeals to me and he is going to get somewhere. Enthusiasm gets me so excited about what I can do that I do not need to worry about what anybody else is doing.

3. **Enthusiasm makes me a positive person.** I have seen people really get the spirit of enthusiasm in their hearts, and they forget about their critics and begin to boost themselves and build up their ability. This applies to a town, a nation, an organization, and even one's personal life. When you get enthusiastic, you forget even your own faults and you begin to think of your powers.

4. **Enthusiasm makes us loyal to the highest things that we believe in.** When people are enthusiastic, they want to do their best and be their best and they begin looking to see what the

best is. Enthusiasm creates lively interest which leads to action.

5. **Enthusiasm will cause one to pay the price.** Most good things in life do not come cheaply. A price must be paid. Sometimes it is the sweat of our brows, sometimes it's working late in the night, sometimes it's giving ourselves to the highest power and not being satisfied with anything less.

6. **The best thing about enthusiasm is it will make us pray.** We never pray until we have something to pray for. As long as we are all that we want to be, have everything we want to have, have done everything we want to do, then there is no need to pray. But when there is something out yonder to touch and we reach as far as we can, then we extend ourselves through the power of prayer.

Living in a world like this ought not to be a dull experience. We all need to get enthusiastic.

SECTION SEVEN – INVOLVEMENT

We Need Companionship

There are times when human companionship and human emotions are important and essential. Once a prominent man received a high honor. Later he said, "The honor really doesn't mean much to me now. My wife died last year, and now I have nobody to tell it to." Having "somebody to tell it to," somebody to walk with, someone to share your feelings, someone to give you support when you need it, having someone to reach out to you, or someone to whom you can "reach out to" means so very much. To try to walk through life without human companionship can be a very difficult experience. Certainly, it is true we can "walk through the valley" if there is a friend by our side.

All of us pass our lives in search of friendship. Our chief desire is to find somebody who can help us become all that we can be. That is the service of a friend. The person who shuts himself or herself away from the companionship of other people is making a great mistake. There are many ways and many places one can find the companionship of friendly people. The point is to seek out those places and take the initiative.

The most creative constructive power on this earth is the power of love. Love is like a boomerang: Send it forth and it comes back to you with even greater force. There is a poem that tells us, "Give love, and love to your heart will flow, a strength in your utmost need."

Elias Howe, a man broken in health and poverty stricken, felt his life was over. Day by day he watched his wife slowly sewing in order to earn a little money for the next meal. Beyond and above all things, Howe loved his wife, and it hurt him to watch her work so hard. Because of his love for her, he forgot his sick body and began thinking how he might help her. He went to work and, six months later, had completed the first model of his sewing machine. It made him famous and rich, and it also made him well. The power of a great love came back to bless him.

Alexander Graham Bell, a great benefactor of humankind, taught in a school for the deaf. He fell in love and married one of his pupils. She could not hear, and because Bell loved her, he suffered because of her handicap. The consuming passion of his life was to do something to help the one he loved. He decided it would be possible to develop a hearing aid, and he set to work. He never counted the hours he spent working on it; he only knew he wanted to help his wife. In the process of his experimentation, he developed the telephone. The love he gave came back to him as a creative, constructive force.

The very moment you fall in love with a great idea, a great cause, a great purpose, or another person, you become creative. Life takes on new meaning and a new direction. You forget the failures of the past; you develop new faith and new powers. Pessimism, doubt, despair, discouragements, and all your negative attitudes are expelled under the power of a great love.

Don't Be a Holdout

Some years ago a tailor phoned to say that a man had bought me a suit as a gift. When I went down to get measured and to select the cloth, the tailor said, "This man wants you to have the best," and he showed me the most expensive cloth he had. A couple of weeks later the suit was delivered to me.

It fit me perfectly. It was the finest suit I ever had. Never have I been prouder of a suit. But it was so nice that I wanted to wear it only on special occasions. When I went away I never took that suit because I thought it might get worn out. I didn't want to put it in my bag because it might get wrinkled. In fact, there were very few occasions when I wanted to wear my good suit through the nearly ten years I kept it.

One day that same tailor was measuring me for another suit. I said, "You remember that first suit you made for me? I still have it." He said, "You can't wear that suit. It is out of style." Not only was it out of style, but from hanging in my closet so long, it had become badly worn by the hangers. By holding it out, I had lost my good suit. I had saved it to death.

I once had dinner in the home of an elderly lady. Her children were grown and gone; her husband had died and now she was alone. During dinner I commented on the lovely tablecloth. After dinner she opened a large chest and carefully lifted out some of the most exquisite linens I have ever seen.

She told me that when she was a young lady, her mother had taught her to sew and had helped to make these lovely things. When she married she had her chest filled, originally called a "Hope chest." I asked, "When do you use these lovely things?" Rather sadly she replied, "I never have used

them. Now it is too late; the one I made them for is gone."
She lost her lovely things by saving them.

When I first began giving talks and writing articles, I had difficulty finding enough material to say or write. I spoke of this to a friend who had been preaching a long time. During our conversation, I told him of a very fine parable I had read. He said, "Why don't you use that in your next article?" I replied, "I am saving that for a special occasion." Then my friend gave me the best lesson I ever received in the art of writing or speaking. He said; "Use everything you have in your next article or speech; then you will find something else." Saving is a virtue that may become a fault. Don't be a hold-out.

A young woman who is near and dear to me recently went to another city to begin a new job. She wanted to make good, and we talked about it. I told her not to worry about how much she was paid or how soon she would get a raise nor to worry about her position. If she were told to sweep the floor, she should sweep it the best it has ever been swept. I told her to forget her own pleasure and give herself to her work, knowing that if she follows that path, she will find the life she really wants.

We could all be happier and accomplish so much more if we weren't afraid to turn loose and give our best. I got a letter from a lady who said that for some years she had wanted to give 10% of her income to charities of her choice, but she didn't have the courage. Finally she did take the plunge and started giving a tenth of her income. She told me what a great joy it has brought to her life.

A mother remembered when her children were little. She stood them on a high place, held out her arms, and told them to jump to her one by one. Each child leapt forward into space. Of course, she could have stepped back and let the child fall and get hurt. But the child never imagined she would do such a thing. Her children had faith in her and knew that her arms would catch them and hold them.

Each of us must preserve that faith. Give yourself away. Don't be a holdout.

Let People Know You Care

Some time ago, I received an anonymous letter which contained these words. I do not know whether they were original or not. I wish I knew how to get in touch with the person who sent it. In reading this, I know these words express the feeling of people all around us.

I cry out in vain.
I look and no one sees.
I speak and no one listens.
I think and no one understands.
I love and no one cares.
I exist and no one knows.
Must I bear this insanity alone?
The ones I care for most could care less.
This life – must I live this Hell?
And yet life goes on.

I tread where no one dares to go.
I border on insanity.
And the sane seem insane.
Has all the world lost all sense of direction?
I offer myself as a sacrifice –
And no one accepts the challenge.
Will those who care come forth?
And love me.

With no love I shall surely perish.
God forbid.

Through the years I have spent countless hours counseling troubled people. Over and over, I have begun those counseling sessions with these words, "Tell me your situation." Most of the time, this is all a person needs – that is, somebody who will listen and let them talk about their lives. There are vast numbers of people who believe that nobody is interested in them. My suggestion to many people who feel defeated and useless in life is that they begin taking an interest in somebody else.

Mr. Sam Rayburn was Speaker of the United States House of Representatives longer than any other man in our history. There is a story about him that reveals the kind of man he really was.

The teenage daughter of a friend of his died suddenly one night. Early the next morning the man heard a knock on his door and when he opened it, there was Mr. Rayburn standing outside. The Speaker said, "I just came by to see what I could do to help." The father replied in his deep grief, "I don't think there is anything you can do, Mr. Speaker. We are making all the arrangements." "Well," Mr. Rayburn said, "Have you had your coffee this morning?"

The man replied that they had not taken time for breakfast. So Mr. Rayburn said that he could at least make coffee for them. While he was working in the kitchen, the man came in and said, "Mr. Speaker, I thought you were supposed to be having breakfast at the White House this morning." "Well, I was," Mr. Rayburn said, "but I called the President and told him I had a friend who was in trouble, and I couldn't come."

I love the humorous tale about a mother who was telling her six year-old about the Golden Rule. "Always remember," she said, "that we are here to help others." The youngster mulled this over for a minute and then asked, "Well, what are the others here for?"

Time and again, there are people in our lives whose problems we cannot solve, but there is something we can do. There is marvelous power that comes back to us when we begin doing something for somebody else.

The Rewards of Giving

What are our motives for giving? Giving is a blessed thing, but often we receive no reward for our giving because we do it for the wrong reason. Sometimes we give because we are in a situation where we are forced into doing so. Other times people give to enhance their own prestige and position. As T. S. Eliot so poignantly says in *Murder in the Cathedral,*

> The last temptation is the greatest treason:
> To do the right deed for the wrong reason.

There is really only one true motive for giving. We give because of the love within our hearts, and love always expresses itself. Giving with the right motive does bring rewards.

First, through giving, we gain a sense of living. What are the greatest joys that parents receive? Is it not in sacrificing for their children? At times, some parents may feel that they are burdened by the things they have to give their child and do for their child. But suppose that child developed an illness and died? As the parents watched the last breath go out of that child, and realized they could do nothing more for the child, actually a part of the life of the mother and the father would die, too. The opportunity to give is really the opportunity to live.

Whenever an opportunity to give is presented to you, be thankful, because that opportunity is opening channels of life to you. The parish priest in A. S. M. Hutchinson's *The Uncertain Trumpet* said it beautifully: "You do not love the life down here because, as you say, you are living for it . . . because when you are here, you are giving; and because life, real life, living, is giving. When you are taking, only taking, you are not living, you are slowly dying."

The second reward of giving is that it strengthens our own lives. One never gives without receiving something more valuable in return. Conversely, to face a situation in which one ought to give, and to turn away from it, brings hurt upon that person. This is true of every duty of life, and certainly giving is one of life's duties. When I face up to my duty and respond to it at my best, I am going to be strengthened by it. When I turn away from a duty, then I am going to be weakened by the very act of turning away.

We must not assume that we should give because it is our duty. As I have indicated, there are higher motives for giving. But, at the same time, we must also recognize that the demands of living carry with them the demands of giving.

We give because we love. But, on the other hand, sometimes giving is the pathway to love. We are familiar with the three rules of giving that have been quoted many, many times: (1) Give, (2) Give until it hurts, (3) Give until it feels good.

Third, one of the great rewards of giving is that it broadens and lengthens our own lives. By giving, I am enabled to serve in many places and in many situations in which I could not expect to be physically present.

In his book *In Quest of a Kingdom*, Leslie D. Weatherhead tells a powerful story:

> "The chairman of a missionary meeting claimed he was the founder of a flourishing Christian community in India, although he had never been out of England. To the amazed listeners, he said that when he was five years old, he wanted to give a penny to the missionaries, but strongly objected to putting it in a brown box. He had no proof

that it ever went abroad. The local minister was a friend of the family and also a friend of an Indian missionary. So the minister, to please the child, sold him a copy of the New Testament for his penny and directed the boy how to post it to the missionary in India, having first written on the flyleaf an inscription giving the name of the boy. The missionary gave it to a poor native who had walked miles through the jungle to procure a testament, but who couldn't afford to buy one.

Nothing was heard of the incident for twenty years. Then, another missionary, preaching in a jungle village to the people whom he thought had never previously heard the gospel message, noticed that his words were causing excited delight. Pausing in his preaching to ask questions, the preacher found that the people knew a great deal about Christ and that many were serving Him. No preacher had ever been to the village before. The little Christian community had been born through the love and life of the native who had been given the Testament – the Testament which was sold for a penny to a child of five."

Giving with the right motive brings great and lasting rewards.

Something To Live For

I heard of the case histories of two women who had almost identical operations. One of the women was a shy, sensitive, overprotected person. The operation was very successful but the lady was constantly depressed. She talked incessantly of "the terrible thing" which had happened to her. She talked about how she would never be able to take care of herself. Three or four weeks after the operation she died.

The other woman had exactly the same operation. However, her surgery was postponed until two weeks after her baby was born. Two weeks after the operation she was at home and soon was completely recovered. She had no time to lie around and feel sorry for herself. She had a baby who needed her. The deepest feeling she had was her love for her baby. A perfect definition of love is difficult to write, but the love of a mother for her baby is the best example of perfect love that I know. Her love cast out all her fear and instead of dying, as did the first woman, she was quickly healed.

There was another girl who was brought to a hospital and died a short time later. Following the autopsy the coroner told the girl's mother, "We could find no cause of death." The mother replied, "Oh, doctor, you don't have to tell me why she died. She died of a broken heart. The young man she was engaged to was killed a few weeks ago. Since then she has had no interest in anything."

"Of a broken heart" – that means she had lost her love. Very often the loss of love means the loss of security, maybe the loss of self-respect. Frequently when love is crushed, one becomes overwhelmed with the feeling of being not needed or not wanted. That can be and often is, fatal. It can destroy any desire to live and, consciously or subconsciously, can create a desire for death. The desire for death becomes stronger than the instinct for self-preservation. Thus it is possible to die of a broken heart.

In my own counseling of many unhappy people who feel defeated and who have given up on life (and given up on themselves), I have suggested they take a sheet of paper and begin writing down some of the reasons for living. We give up and quit because there is no reason for living. Finding a reason for living immediately gives new power. The best nerve medicine on this earth is a life purpose.

George Bernard Shaw suggested that an appropriate epitaph for a lot of people would be "died at thirty, buried at sixty." In contrast, I like the spirit of one of my elderly hospice patients who said, "I am going to live until I die, and then I am going to live forever." A lot of people worry about the wrong thing. They worry about life after death when they ought to be worrying about life after birth. If people are properly concerned about living, then they are not improperly worried about eternity.

> To look up and not down,
> To look forward and not back,
> To look out and not in, and
> To lend a hand.

George Bernard Shaw also once described a certain person as "a selfish little clod of ailments and grievances, complaining that the world will not devote itself to making him happy." Unselfish service to others can turn even the utmost tragedy into victory. Let's remember well this truth — happy people are helpful people.

When you give yourself to something greater than yourself, when some great cause becomes more important than your own life, and to that cause you give all of your interests and feelings, then that cause will give back to you a stronger and healthier life than you ever experienced before. Self-centeredness makes us sick. Perfect love heals us.

Really Listening and Developing Ourselves

Do you feel that people seek your friendship and involvement? This is a very important question. Many people feel overlooked and left out. We need to emphasize the fact that the secret to being interesting is to be interested. Quit worrying about people's being interested in you, and start working to develop your own interests, as much as you possibly can.

We all know people who are interested only in themselves. In conversation, whatever subject you mention, this person is quick to top whatever you said with their experience. If you refer to a trip you took, the moment you pause, this person begins telling of a trip they took. If you tell of a family member, as soon as this person gets a chance, they start telling you about a member of their family, and so on. You get the idea they are not interested in anything but themselves and their own concerns. These people are usually avoided by others.

We can all remember times when we made mistakes, but happily we can also remember times when we did the right thing. Such a time happened to my wife and me. We had dinner with a couple who had recently been to Europe. They were obviously excited about their trip. It was their first trip out of the country, and the first long plane ride. During our dinner and for almost an hour afterward, they told us every detail about their trip and we listened – at times with interest and at times with boredom – but we listened, and we were very pleased with ourselves that we did.

It would have been so easy for us to break in and say, "Let us tell you about the last time we were in Europe." But, they wanted somebody to listen, while they told us about the trip of their lives. And, we really did find it interesting to see what a couple would say about their first trip abroad.

Parents need to remind themselves constantly that children need to be listened to. A father once told me of an experience with his son. His son had finished college and had gone to work in a large corporation. In his work he was having some difficulties adjusting to his fellow workers, as well as learning his job. One night the son said to his father, "I wish you would give me some advice about my situation at work." The father told me that for almost two hours the boy sat and talked to him about both the problems and the possibilities in his situation. Patiently, and with genuine interest, that father listened as the boy talked. Finally the boy finished and said to his father, "You have really helped me tonight and I feel everything is going to work out fine."

The father hardly said a word, but sometimes listening is more powerful than speaking. Listening to a person is the very essence of counseling. Most people do not want you to give them advice. They want you to listen to their ideas. If you are willing to listen, you have laid the foundation of lasting friendship.

The trouble with many people is that they have never extended their interest beyond themselves. How much time and effort do you give in developing your interests? Here's a brief list of guidelines for getting along with other people:

1. Be interested in the happiness and well-being of other people, and be sympathetic to the hurts and problems of others.
2. Learn peoples' names.
3. Do not speak with an uncontrolled temper.
4. Be careful to greet people when greeting is in order.
5. Be slow to condemn, quick to praise.
6. Be willing to give more than ask from others.
7. Forgive and be willing to ask for forgiveness.

8. Believe that you are making some important contribution to life.
9. Believe that each person you meet is making some important contribution to life.
10. Remember, no person is big enough to cause you to hate.
11. When disagreements arise, do not concentrate on placing blame, but rather, concentrate on communication.
12. Seek to understand the right action in each situation – and then do it.

A good habit to develop is to regularly take pencil and paper and make a list of your interests. And remember this: as you broaden your interests, you will find more people interested in you.

PART EIGHT – LOVE

What We Need Is Love

A woman asked her husband to care for their children one Saturday afternoon while she went shopping. He happened to be a statistician. When she returned, he handed her a record of the afternoon:

Dried the children's tears – 14 times
Tied their shoe laces – 16 times
Served drinks of water – 22 times
Toy balloons blown up – 3 per child
Average life of balloon – 12 seconds
Warned children not to cross the street – 34 times
Children insisted on crossing street – 34 times
Number of Saturdays I will do this in the future – NONE

I sympathize with the poor fellow. For most parents, there is no sweeter hour than when they finally get their children to sleep and can sit down and rest for a little while. But it is simply a fact that many times we give children everything – except the most important, ourselves. Missing that one thing, they miss everything.

If love is given to a child as the child has a right to expect, that child may be punished for wrongs committed, denied many other advantages, even perhaps an education, yet that child receiving love will grow to be a happy and emotionally well-balanced child.

A father once told me about one of his boys coming into his study one day while he was very busy. He suggested his son amuse himself in a number of ways, but the boy kept refusing. Exasperated he asked, "Son, what do you want?" The boy replied, "Daddy, I just want you."

I tell that not as a sentimental story. Rather it illustrates the most basic desire of a child, and, missing that "you," the child misses everything. That also explains why there are so many maladjusted people today. No amount of fame or public applause ever takes the place of warm, genuine human love.

The love-starved person may turn to misanthropy, which is a dislike or distrust of humankind. The same person may spend his life in a false philanthropy, claiming to love humankind and rendering all manner of services for the betterment of people, when all the time, he or she is not concerned with helping others; they are merely seeking a substitute for love missed.

Study, for example, the writings and life of Hitler. He screamed with evangelical fervor his desires to put bread into the mouths of hungry people, when all the time, he was really seeking to build up his own love-starved ego. All his talk about a master race was merely a screen behind which he was seeking the glory of others for himself.

There was a woman who twice had been committed to an institution for the mentally ill. Fearing another breakdown, she decided to go back to the small town of her girlhood for a visit. She had not been back since she first went away to college. She spent the summer there with an old lady who had known her family since before she was born. The old woman told her much family history – how she was an unwanted child, treated coldly. "I used to feel so sorry for you when you were a little tyke. A child needs love if it is to grow right, just as an adult must have love to keep sane."

This opened a new world of fact for the woman and sent her searching for more facts. She learned there can be no growth without love. She learned that when one selects a life of lonely selfishness that one is also cutting off the warm mental stimulation which gives zest to living. The wise old woman convinced her that she would never lose her mind if she surrounded herself with loving and caring people. Then the elder told her to substitute thoughts of helping others for her fear of another mental breakdown. As she learned to love, the woman became a sane, balanced, and well person.

That is the pathway for one to follow who has been love-starved. I have talked with many people privately who are literally starving for love. They are bitter and resentful. Some have the spirit of Frederick the Great. One day he struck a subject with a whip and exclaimed: "Confound you: I want you to love me." But love is not something which can be commanded.

A definition of love which years ago won a national newspaper contest reads: "Love is the doorway through which the human soul passes from selfishness to service and from solitude to kinship with all." There is only one way to make up for the love you missed: that one way is loving.

How Do We Love?

We all talk about what love is. Perhaps we can say a few things about what love is not and better discover how we best love one another.

Recognition is not love. It is important to recognize a person as a human being and to recognize a person's accomplishment and place in society. Being ignored or overlooked is a difficult experience to bear. Yet recognizing is not the same as loving.

There are some people who feel that it is better to be treated badly than to be ignored. Across the years, I have talked with both wives and husbands who were abused by their spouses. They did not get a divorce because at least they were being recognized by the other – but they were not being loved.

On the other hand, positive attention may not be love. A husband may phone his wife five times a day from the office. He may bring flowers, candy, and gifts. He may give her all manner of attention, but still not love her. And, vice versa, the wife may prepare just the meals that he wants, constantly compliment him and do all the things that he wants – and still not love him.

I heard a father say to a son sometime ago, "When you consider all that I have given to you in the last three years, how could you doubt that I love you?" This father is making a very big mistake. There is a vast difference in giving and loving. One can give to satisfy his or her own ego, to salve a guilty conscience, or even as a substitute for love.

Neither is love looking up to a person adoringly. We all like to be admired. When someone gives us special attention, it is easy to respond happily and enthusiastically. But being admired is not being loved.

We hear the expression, "Love at first sight." I have always thought that was a contradiction in terms. Love is a growing, developing experience. Sexual desire can come at first sight. Infatuation can be a first sight experience, but love is a long term relationship.

Not even sharing is love. Love may involve sharing, but not necessarily so. Two people can hope, dream, aspire, and work together without loving each other.

Love includes, to some degree, all of the above, but love goes beyond all of the above. If one really wants to know what love is, then I suggest the reading of the Thirteenth Chapter of First Corinthians. That is the best definition I know. How do we love one another? The following anonymous passage I have seen in countless church bulletins and inspirational leaflets tells us:

> I was hungry
>> And you formed a humanities club
>> And you discussed my hunger.
>> Thank you.
>
> I was imprisoned
>> And you crept off quietly
>> To your chapel in the cellar
>> And prayed for my release.
>
> I was naked
>> And in your mind
>> You debated the morality of my
>> Appearance.
>
> I was sick
>> And you knelt and thanked God
>> For your health.

I was homeless
    And you preached to me
    Of the spiritual shelter of the
    Love of God.

I was lonely
    And you left me alone
    To pray for me.

You seem so holy:
    So close to God
    But I'm still very hungry
    And lonely
        And cold.

So where have your prayers gone?
What have they done?
What does it profit a man to page through his
book of prayers
When the rest of the world is crying for help?

A great American storyteller wrote about two young people who were very much in love. Christmas Eve was coming and they wanted to give presents to one another. But they were very poor and had no money for presents. So each one, without telling the other, decided to sell his or her most precious possession. The woman's most precious possession was her long golden hair. She went to a hairdresser, had it cut off and sold it to buy a lovely watch chain for her lover's watch. He, meanwhile, had gone to a jeweler and sold his watch to buy two beautiful combs for his beloved's hair. Then they exchanged their gifts. There were tears at first and then laughter. There was no hair for the combs and no watch for the watch chain. But there was something more precious and that was their self-sacrificing love for one another.

The Eight Be-Attitudes of Marriage

My wife Kathy and I were married on February 17, 1990. During our sacramental celebration we expressed to one another and to the congregation our "eight be-attitudes of marriage."

What really makes a marriage work? Marriage is far too complex for one simple answer or secret.

1. **Enjoy one another.** It is important to laugh, to touch, to pray, to enjoy sexuality, and to make life exciting for one another. Look for the humor and fun of life. So many are bored because there is no humor. See God in the other without expecting your spouse to act like God.

2. **Have the ability to change.** Keep adapting to make the marriage work. Success in marriage is more than finding the right person: it is a matter of being the right person. Be open to change and growth.

3. **Have the ability to live with the unchangeable.** You have to know when to holler and when to look away. We laugh when Rodney Dangerfield gets no respect. In relationships, it is vital that we give respect and reverence. In marriage, it's a must. There are many elements we cannot control in the other.

4. **Marriage means permanence.** Forever is an ongoing philosophy. Forever is a long time. Treat each other with kindness, encouragement, and challenge. Marriage is the commitment of two people as total persons.

5. **Trust each other.** This is the basis for marital intimacy. Schedule leisurely breaks for

conversation. There are 168 hours and 10,080 minutes each week. The average couple only spends 17 minutes per week in conversation. Share the pleasant and the unpleasant.

6. **Marriage is a balance of dependencies**. It is necessary to depend upon your spouse. We need to be a mixture of dependent, independent, and interdependent. Seek to meet your partner's basic needs.

7. **Realize you have a shared and cherished history**. As a couple you have a real history. Remember your first date. Recall your engagement. Watch your wedding video and review your wedding album together. Look forward to each anniversary. Become historical and not hysterical.

8. **Remember that the Lord is always with you**. After our scripture readings we responded: "Thanks be to God!" On our wedding day we pledged to say "Thanks be to God" every day for the gift of one another. We promised to pray daily for our life together.

Our deepest advice is not to marry someone you can live with. Marry someone you cannot live without. There's a big difference. You are made to love and to be loved.

PART NINE - JOY, BEAUTY AND WONDER

Recover Your Sense of Wonder

We need to recover our sense of wonder, our anticipation of the glorious, our relationship with something or someone that "turns us on." Thomas Carlyle once said, "The person who cannot wonder . . . is but a pair of spectacles behind which there is no eye." Everyone of us needs to retain that something within us that can exclaim, "Wow! Isn't that wonderful!"

Too many of us look at life with a mere, "Ho hum." We live in a world of constant miracles. You can pick up your phone and talk to somebody on the other side of the world; you can get in an airplane and in a matter of hours fly over the Atlantic, which took Columbus months to cross; you can go to a hospital and see miraculously healed people walking out; you can talk to individuals who have literally walked on the moon. Miracles are all about us, so much that we reach the place where they simply do not excite us or inspire us.

"The most beautiful experience we can have," wrote Albert Einstein, "is the mysterious. It is the fundamental emotion which stands at the cradle of true art and true science." We must allow for the mystery. We must accept the mystery. We must be a part of the mystery. We must be encompassed by the mystery. What is not mystery?

Stand in reverent respect before that which inspires you. Feel new strength and power; and then, in the name of the highest and the holiest, get going.

Consider the Heavens

Have you ever wondered why the world is so beautiful, so impressive, and so big? Nobody knows how big the heavens are with it's millions, maybe billions of stars. Why is it that every morning the glory of a sunrise comes over the earth and every evening the quiet beauty of a sunset? It could have been arranged so the day would come and go in a less impressive manner.

Have you ever looked at a great mountain range and wondered why the peaks are so high? Mountains aren't really good for anything. They could have been left out. They can't be cultivated; and beyond a certain point, they don't even grow trees. We do not need mountains in order to live on this earth.

I have flown across the trackless deserts of the West. As I looked at the endless miles of hot sand, I wondered why they were that way. The deserts aren't good for anything. No food can grow there; the few creatures who live there are worthless to humankind.

I am most impressed when I look at the ocean. Nobody really knows how big the ocean is. In places it is literally miles deep. It seems an awful waste. Rain could still exist without creating that vast reservoir of water. Why do we have an ocean?

The tragedy is that many people live surrounded by creation and never consider it. A thoughtless person once said to Helen Keller, "Isn't it awful to be blind?" She replied, "Not half so bad as to have two good eyes and never see anything." And there are people who are content with a mighty small world. They never "consider the heavens." They never really see anything big.

I have watched colossal storms roar across the mountains. Heavy clouds come thundering in and everything gets dark. You begin to wonder if the world isn't going to be destroyed. Then the clouds break up and you see the green mountainside bathed in sunlight. And you know that if you wait out the storm, there will be sunlight again. When we have trouble and everything seems lost, with a picture of the greatness of all creation in mind, we gain courage and calmness.

On the other hand, when the sun is shining and the breezes are gentle, we know it will not always remain so. Sooner or later it will cloud up again. So we make preparations during the good weather for the bad that is sure to follow. Likewise, when we are blessed with a life that is smooth and good, we remember that we must be ready for the trouble that is sure to come. Realizing the greatness of creation, our minds are stretched to take the long view of life, not living just for the moment but considering the whole.

All of us have an amazing capacity for growth. We begin to touch new possibilities of growth by traveling to new and exciting places and lands. I have seen magnificent creations through travel: the Canadian Rockies, the Isle of Capri, the Grand Canyon, the great cathedrals of Europe, and the Rock of Gibraltar to mention a few. There are many places I would like to see – Vienna, Australia, Yellowstone National Park, the Greek Isles, to mention a few.

Consider the heavenly places you can go through the many excursions available to you. It's a chance of a lifetime to stretch your vision, your mind and your soul. Happy trails!

Laughter, Wonder and Delight

Laughter is one of the best forms of relaxation. Laughing stirs up the blood, expands the chest, electrifies the nerves, clears away the cobwebs from the brain, and gives your whole system a cleansing rehabilitation.

One human question we puzzle over is: Why are there so many vivacious and brilliant children and so many "dull" adults? The loss of the sense of laughter, wonder, and delight has something to do with this decline to dullness.

1. So often we are people imprisoned within our souls. I believe there are four prison cells of our spirits: So many lives are cramped and heavy laden by drudgery. Every preacher who has ever lived has told this same story. Three men were working at the task of laying brick. One of those men was saying, "I have to lay so many bricks a day." The second man was saying, "I am earning so many dollars per day." The third man was saying, "I am helping to build a great cathedral." A high and holy purpose takes us out of the prison of drudgery.

2. Another prison of our spirits is possessions. Many people rather than possessing things, are possessed by things. Some tribes in Africa used to catch monkeys in the trees by taking a gourd and cutting a hole in the gourd, just large enough for a monkey to put his hand into. In the gourd they put some nuts and tie the gourd securely in a tree. The monkey would put his hand in the gourd and take

hold of the nuts, but in doubling up his fist he could not get his hand out of the small hole. The monkey was not willing to let go of the nuts; therefore he was trapped, and the natives could easily capture him. He was imprisoned by things.

3. The third prison is a feeling of guilt. I would like to dedicate my entire life to telling people no matter what you have done, God still loves you, He will wipe the slate clean, and you can start over again. Not far from New York City there is a grave. On the stone of that grave is just one word – "forgiven." There is no name, no date and no other description. That stone speaks to every one of us. It does not matter who you are, when or where you live; the word "forgiven" can be written over your life.

4. The last prison is the fear of death. It is normal to want to live, but it is abnormal to live in fear of death. One thing we can be certain about is that we are going to die. So why worry about it; why not live the best we can and accept death when it comes.

Let's keep our lives wonder-ful and delight-ful. Let's practice laughing when we're alone. A loud "ha, ha, ha" while we're driving can startle us at first. We don't have to be comedians to be able to laugh. All we have to do is want to see the other side of life – the humorous side. Let's fill our world with laughter, wonder, and delight. It's contagious!

The Joy of Swimming

I find great joy in swimming and was an ardent member of Lakeside Swim Club for years. Swimming is definitely one of the cleanest sports (you're not sweaty when you finish). It's an activity you can do straight through your senior years without having to worry about excessive strain on an aging body. It doesn't take very much equipment or preparation. There's no suffering with blistered feet or twisted ankles, swollen wrists or painful elbows. I find fun, pleasure, relaxation, and inner peace in swimming a half mile to a mile, rain or shine, summer and winter, three to five times a week.

Swimming is a perfect activity for the high-pressured, competitive twenty-first century. It's a sport to ease the mind, to release daily tensions, and to develop the body free from the demands of the battleground most of us call our lives and careers.

Ocean water covers two-thirds of the earth's surface. The Greek philosopher, Thales, theorized that water was the earth's primal substance, source of all things including air, earth – even fire. Water is abundant and incredibly varied: cold makes it solid snow or ice; heat vaporizes it into steam. Essential in nutrition, vital in industry as a catalyst and solvent, water allows transportation, cooling, disposal, cleansing, and power. It is a standard of scientific measurement, a concrete instance for important physical units and properties like calories, specific gravity and relative viscosity. Ritual washing is a feature in many religions. Even modern rites center on immersion. What does swimming in this amazing substance do for the inner you?

1. **It will relax you.** Any tense or emotionally charged situation will often arouse cries of "cool it," "stay cool," or "keep cool." In swimming you make real those figurative expressions. The combined effects of the water and the regular rhythmical action of the swim create a restfulness unlike any you can experience elsewhere.

2. **It will bring you solitude.** In swimming there is opportunity for total solitude and freedom. The restrictions of the swim force your mind inward; alone with yourself, you confront your inner being. You are free to think, and the comfort of the water makes even those thoughts you may hate to face somehow easier to deal with.

3. **It will give you a new confidence in yourself.** From swimming you will receive a confidence that grows from the pride of achievement plus the confidence you feel knowing that you're keeping your body fit and toned. You'll have reserves of energy.

4. **It will bring an element of play into your life.** Swimming as children we all splashed and played and lost ourselves in water under the sun – the memories of those days, rekindled by swimming as adults, restore us to childhood joy and delight.

5. **It will enhance your creativity.** The water has a mysterious effect upon the mental process, upon perception and creativity. You're not just thinking – you're thinking better, clearer, and sharper than you ever have before. Most of my ideas for writing come

while swimming. Most of the solutions to my daily dilemmas come during a swim.

6. **It will put you in touch with the elements of nature.** "I love the feel of water on my body," one woman swimmer told me. When you immerse yourself and swim you are touching your own origins, water swirling about you, water that represents nature, religion, birth, and survival. You feel a harmony of being as you make direct contact with life's most basic element.

The remarkable thing to consider about swimming as you age is that you will never have to stop swimming. In *Sports in America* James Michener offers an interesting table in which he lists selected sports recommended according to a persons age. Each decade of life from five to eight-five has three groups of activities: "highly recommended," "worth investigating," and "demanding but possible." Swimming appears on the table in the "highly recommended" column for the first decade, ages five to fifteen; and it stays in that column for six of the remaining seven decades. Michener shifted swimming to the "worth investigating" column for the seventy-five to eight-five year olds.

One fellow at the swim club wouldn't appreciate the subtle shift. Now in his 70s, he intends to swim forever. "I'll never stop. I want them to carry me from the pool to the grave," he said with a smirk. "And when I'm six feet under I'll look up and say 'Forget the dirt. Just add water.'"

PART TEN – HAPPINESS

The Beauty of Life

An old story tells of two men who were walking along the streets of London when the music of some grand chimes in a nearby cathedral floated through the air.

One of them remarked to the other, "Isn't that wonderful music?" "I didn't hear what you said," replied the other. "Aren't those chimes beautiful?" repeated the first man. But again the other man failed to catch the words, and the first speaker said for the third time, "Isn't that lovely music?" "It's no use," came the answer, "those pesky bells are making so much noise that I can't hear a word you're saying."

We hear that to which we attune ourselves, and usually we attune ourselves to what we wish to hear. Bias and selfishness warp the lives of countless people. The world contains discordant notes; it also contains sweet harmony.

Each person catches for themselves what they set out to catch. The difference in the quality of our lives is the difference in how we attune ourselves to the world around us. Each of us is in charge of our own destiny. Ringing bells can be a joy to our hearts or they can be an annoying interference in life.

We are free to accept the beautiful, the artistic, and the charming things in life that bring joy to our hearts, that enlighten our minds and make life beautiful. It can be accomplished by filling our minds with ennobling and beautiful thoughts – by being positive, by positive thinking and by planning each day in a beautiful way. Helen Keller was once asked what she thought to be the worst calamity that might befall a person. She answered, "To have eyes and fail to see."

Why don't we remind ourselves more often that we have the priceless gift of eyesight and determine to use it better? Famous photographers have a talent for finding beauty, excitement, even drama in their perception of what we call "little everyday things." When we see their pictures, we find ourselves charmed, or touched, or delighted by the unexpected perspective to a special element that we might have overlooked entirely.

Why don't we train ourselves to use our eyes as the photographer uses his view finder? Why not look a bit more closely to see the wealth of beauty that surrounds us? The world is too big to be taken in at one glance. We must look again and again to find the fascinating details that we miss if our first glance is too quick or too casual. We must use imagination to develop a way of seeing that Ernest Haas, a famous photographer, calls "dreaming with one's eyes open."

Children have the ability to see beauty that adults lose as they get older. After a rain a little girl said to her mother, "Oh, look, Mommy, there's a rainbow in the gutter!" "That's not a rainbow, silly," her mother corrected. "That's a dirty oil slick." Perhaps if we could continue to see as a child, we would never have to say that we're bored or that nothing ever happens.

Let's appreciate the lovely tapestry of life through our eyes. It's so easy to look up to see a snow capped mountain, and to look downward, too, to see the first crocus of spring half hidden in the snow.

One day in mid-winter, I got caught in a blizzard walking down the street where I lived. As I rounded the corner I came upon an old friend. He was warmly clothed, apparently very comfortable, and leaning on his cane. He offered his usual greeting, "Hey Bob, it's a fine day, isn't it?" At that moment I didn't agree and spoke my mind saying, "What do you mean, calling this a fine day?" The old man straightened a little and said, "Well, it's the finest day of its kind I ever saw."

This is a wonderful story, because it explains positive thinking to us in a few short sentences. Anyone who reaches success in any shape or form, either materially or spiritually, is a positive thinker. This old man was an outstanding positive thinker. Let's imitate his zeal and always look forward to everything we do with a positive attitude, truly believing that even the worst can turn out to be beautiful.

Signs of a Happy Person

I would say, "Miserable are the people who do not have something beyond themselves to search for." Searching means keeping on the move.

A dairy farmer in Glendale, Kentucky told me he happily remembered the days when he could dip water out of a running stream in the nearby mountains and drink it without fear. The running water in the mountain streams was constantly purifying itself. If the water reached a place where it quit moving, only then would it become stagnant and begin to develop impurities.

Many of us can testify to the fact that one of life's most difficult experiences is facing the death of a loved one. When it comes, what do you do? You certainly need to grieve. After a while, though, you can sit around mourning, or you can get up and get going. Again and again, we find people whose lives reached their heights as they became active in the midst of a great sorrow.

The kind of people I like best and I suspect you do too, are the "How are you?" type people. That is, people who give me the feeling that they are not thinking about themselves, but for now at least, their fist concern is for me. As somebody reaches out in warmth and interest to another, in the very reaching, he finds joy and satisfaction.

On the other hand, the people most of us dislike are the "What's in it for me?" folks. These "me-first" people never **feel** warmth coming from any other person. They will never find happiness when their favorite charity is themselves. Many people blame others for their mistakes. When they are alone and lonely, it is too easy for them to say that everyone else is marching off in the wrong direction, and only they are going in the right direction.

The people who forget themselves while thinking of others are the ones who say, "Let's go!" They never lack for fellowship or for friendship. The "me first" people are the ones who always end up being left out of the fellowship and miss out on uplifting friendships.

Happy people enjoy their relationships with other people. The unhappy people dislike their work and their world. Sooner or later, they dissipate their talents and their gifts. Not finding satisfaction in their work, they are never inspired to be or to do their best. Fault finding is the number one temptation of unhappy people. Out of that comes jealousy, self-deprecation, and even self-hatred.

Recently, I went to see a small child who was a patient in the hospital. It was approaching eight o'clock in the evening when I went into the room. There, beside the child's bed was her mother. I asked her if she had eaten dinner, and she replied that she had not. Then I asked her if she had eaten lunch, and again her reply was that she had not. What had happened was that she was so concerned for her little girl, that she forgot about her own hunger and her own needs. When we find something important enough to give our full attention to, we quit worrying about our own problems.

Let me sum up some of the signs of a happy person — those who take life "for gratitude" and not "for granted."

- The happy person lives by affirmations rather than denunciations.
- The happy person sees good in others.
- The happy person gives wholehearted effort to an undertaking. Loafing never leads to happiness.
- The happy person is always eager to give, and is also willing to receive.

- The happy person knows that life is too short to be unhappy. Those who have experienced happiness universally testify that the other problems of life either disappear or else are solved.
- Finally, for the happy individual the problems of life are changed into challenges and opportunities.

Which of these signs are visible in your life? You too can choose to be happy.

PART ELEVEN – PEACE

A Place of Warmth and Rest

One of the greatest losses we Americans have suffered is the old-fashioned fireplace. Several generations ago, folks would gather around after supper, put two or three fresh logs into the fireplace, and sit there basking in the warmth and watching the flames dance up and the red coals slowly turning into ashes. There was no radio, and no light to read by, so they would just sit there an hour or so and talk a little, but mostly just sit and think about things, slowly rocking in the old rocking chair. Naturally, a good night's sleep followed such an evening. And the next day, minds were clear and serene.

I am not calling for the "good old days" again. I enjoy living in an automatically gas heated house. Yet one of the fond dreams of my life is to have a little cabin not far away with a wood fireplace where I can go occasionally and just sit, think, watch the fire, and slowly rock. I would be a better man for it.

A man came to see me who said he needed help. I asked him to tell me his story, and he talked for twenty minutes without my saying a word. He was all mixed up in his home life, his personal life, and now his business was almost ruined. I asked, "What do you plan to do?" He thought a few moments and then told me the steps he planned to take. I said, "That sounds like a good plan to me. I don't believe I can suggest anything else." Then he got up and said, "You've solved my problems for me." He thanked me heartily and left.

But I had not solved anything. I had not even said anything. The solutions were entirely his. After he left I sat thinking about this business of personal problems, which all of us have in one form or another.

I remembered when a hurricane was headed toward Florida. The Army Air Corps wanted to conduct some studies of hurricanes and sent a plane out to meet this one. When they got to it, they flew straight into the center. It was the first time any person had ever flown into the center of a hurricane. When they got inside, they found not rain or high winds, but perfect calm. It was so calm and peaceful that they flew around inside for some time. Later, one of them said that he would never be afraid of a hurricane again – if he could only get to the center of it.

I realized that my visitor had done exactly that. He simply sat down and in a calm and orderly way thought and talked himself into the very center of the hurricane of his own life. Then, in such a frame of mind, he could see the way out, and it gave him confidence and peace. I had not done anything for him except be quiet and listen. Any number of his friends could have done the same thing for him. Any number of our friends can do it for us. We can even do it by ourselves.

Thinking about this man who was troubled, and about the old fireside, makes me realize again what so many of us need most. It is a place of quiet rest. If we can just get at the center of these things that upset us so, we would find a calm there and in that calmness, begin to see the way out.

We Americans have the most comfortable homes ever built, the finest beds ever made, luxurious automobiles in which to ride, the most elaborate recreational facilities of all time, and the shortest work week in history. Yet, we are a tired and weary people.

Dante, the Italian poet, when asked by some monks where he was going and what he was seeking, replied, "I am searching for that which every person seeks – peace and rest." Most of us have that same desire deep in our hearts.

If there is one lesson this generation needs to learn, it is how to take time to live. I enjoy watching people in church. Many sit as if they think the pew might fall down. They fret if there is any lost time during the service. They want the service to be short and snappy, and the minute the benediction is pronounced they break for the door like a bunch of motorcycles taking off when a red light has turned to green.

I talk privately with a lot of people, most of whom start the interviews by saying, "I know you are in a hurry." But long ago I learned you cannot counsel people on the run. I tell many that they have already run past far more than they will ever catch up with.

One of my favorite prayers is the prayer for personal peace of Frank Borman of the Apollo 8 mission, first used on Christmas Eve, 1968:

> "Give us, O God, the vision which can see thy love in the world in spite of human failure. Give us the faith, the trust, the goodness in spite of our ignorance and weakness. Give us the knowledge that we may continue to pray with understanding hearts, and show us what each one of us can do to set forth the coming of the day of universal peace."

Twelve Steps to Peace

How can you find peace in the valleys of your life? Here are twelve steps everyone can take.

1. Begin realizing that worry is a habit. Just like any other habit, it can be faced, dealt with, and overcome. Often we do not worry about specific trouble; rather we worry because we have acquired a bad habit.

2. When you are upset, put skid chains on your tongue. Most of us have a tendency to talk too much when we are disturbed. We need to think more and say less.

3. Practice the art of a cheerful countenance. Sometimes it is better to smile than it is to cry. To hide your pains and worries and disappointments under a smile can often lead to a cheerful heart.

4. Go ahead and cry. This is not contradictory to the idea of being cheerful. There are times when we need to cry, sometimes our tears bathe our souls. There are times to hide our emotions and times to express our emotions. We need to be able to know the difference.

5. When you are disturbed and bothered, analyze your problems. It has been said that 40 per cent of the things that disturb us are in the past, 50 per cent are in the future and only 10 per cent are problems we can deal with today. Separate your upsetting thoughts and deal with that 10 per cent you can deal with now.

6. When we are upset, we are tempted to talk about the vices of other people. This is the time to say

nothing, unless we can say something good. Time and again people have made comments they wish they had never made. There are times when saying nothing is the very best course.

7. Sometimes people say unpleasant things about us. In fact this is one of the biggest reasons people get upset and disturbed. I'm not saying we should pay no attention to the remarks of others. There are times when we should consider those statements and ask ourselves if they are justified. If the comments are not valid, there are times when the person who made them should be confronted. However, the time to deal with the unhappy remarks about ourselves is not while we are in the valley.

8. The wisest psychologist America has ever produced was William James. He once said, "The essence of genius is to know what to overlook." There are some things that are just not worth bothering about.

9. Many times we are too self-centered. To develop interest in other people – in what they are doing, in their needs, in their joys and sorrows – brings us great rewards. We need to develop the habit of making everyone we meet, however humble the person may be, know that he or she is important.

10. Never tell a joke at someone else's expense. One of my heroes was Jack Benny. I listened to him often. He made the world laugh, but if you remember, he made the world laugh at him. He never belittled someone else to get a laugh.

11. Stop worrying about whether you have been duly rewarded. Do your work, be patient, keep a

cheerful disposition, and you can be certain that eventually you will receive the respect due you. Don't worry about it; you will be recognized. Believing that, you will be under less stress.

12. Every so often, you need to stop by a gas station and fill up the tank of your car. Otherwise your car will stop running. So it is with the human mind. We need to practice filling our minds with positive thoughts that lead to courage, calmness and joy. Too many of us find ourselves in a valley because we did not stop to fill up our minds.

PEACE!

PART TWELVE – HOPE

Never Despair

There are many people living alone with a gloomy outlook of hopeless despair. They have real difficulty believing that anything good will ever happen in their lives.

I love the story of the priest who became concerned about a poor-looking man he frequently saw sitting in front of the Laundromat. One day the priest put two dollars into this man's hand and whispered the words to him, "Never despair." The next day the man stopped the priest and handed him sixteen dollars. "What is the meaning of this," the priest asked. The man replied, "It means NEVER DESPAIR won the fifth race at Churchill Downs and paid eight to one."

This may not be the most inspiring story in the world, but it does have a point. "Never despair" may pay off more than you think.

We can talk about the future in two very different ways. We can say: (1) "I believe in the future," or (2) "I believe the future in." Study those two sentences. The second sentence is saying that if you believe, you can create a future. There is marvelous power when you start believing.

In "believing your future in" you need to learn to live with some things that cannot be changed. One of the unchangeable things of our lives is our own past. If happy memories come out of your past, it isn't hard to live with those. But it is hard to live with some of the sad memories that bring sorrow or regret.

Sometimes memories of the past destroy our desire to live in the present or to hope for the future. At some time, every one of us has said words to this effect: "If only I could have time to live over again! If only I had done things differently in the past!" The truth is, we just need to accept the fact that the past is a part of us. We cannot deny it, excuse it, or get rid of it.

Concentrate on this glorious thought "You can believe your future in." Some would call it a "new life." It is freeing to realize there will come a day when you look back at next year (I emphasize "next" year) and it will be a new past for you. The point is: we have a past, but we can also create another past. So, let's stop looking back and begin believing our future in.

When a former piano teacher prepared me for my recitals, she would have me practice the final bars over and over again. Invariably her students would grumble because of the repetition of the last few measures of music. When we would complain, our wise teacher would always answer, "You can make a mistake in the beginning or you can make a mistake in the middle. Your audience will forget the mistakes if you make the ending glorious."

Words of Hope

When you become discouraged, when life looks utterly dark, when your plans have failed, then you can take one of three ways out.

First, there is the way of the fool. They say, "This is hopeless, so I'll quit." "I don't like this job; I'll find a new one." "My marriage is not fun any longer; I'll break it up." "I can't face this situation; I'll run away from it." The fool is always quitting and never holding on to hope.

A second way to face the troubles of life is the cynic's way. It is a little better than the fool's way but not much. A cynic believes everything turns out badly. "This is just my luck," they say. "There is no joy in life for me. I'll just bear it as best I can." They never expect much and so they are never disappointed.

A third way to face life is the way of hope. Of course there will be disappointments and setbacks, but hope sees the sunshine coming behind the storm. These people say, "Life is full of glad surprises for those who hope." The great fact to remember is that the trend of civilization itself is forever upward; that a line drawn through the middle of the peaks and valleys of the centuries always has an upward trend. That fact - and it is fact - is always cause for hope.

Tribulation - patience - experience - hope. That is the order in which it comes. If people never had trouble, they would never have any hope. Trouble develops patience, which enables us to bear life as we go on living. As we live we gain experience. As a result of experience in living, we can and do see reason for hope. If we could not look back and see victories gained over adverse circumstances, we would have no hope in the midst of the troubles we are experiencing today, or fear that we might expect tomorrow.

"It is history that teaches us to hope," said Robert E. Lee. That is absolutely true, whether we are seeing history as related to the world and all people, or whether we are looking at history just in relation to our own lives. Memory is a great producer of hope.

Tribulation - patience - experience - hope. Not only in reference to our own personal experiences, but also when we think of the lessons of history, this formula works. It is a discouraging experience to look at all the problems and troubles of the world. "But no man who is correctly informed as to the past," said Thomas Macaulay, "will be disposed to take a morose or desponding view of the present."

As we study history we learn that the pathway of humankind has not been easy. There have been dark periods of war and economic depression. There have been storms, earthquakes, and major catastrophes of all kinds. Disease and hunger have sent so many to early graves. But in spite of everything that has happened, the record of humankind is one of progress. Out of each setback there comes a new beginning and a powerful forward surge.

Hanging in the Tate Gallery in London is George Frederic Watts' great painting entitled "Hope." It pictures a blind-folded woman sitting on the stricken and dejected world. In her hand is a harp with all the strings broken except one. She is striking that one string and her head is bent toward it in closest attention to catch its sound. This is the artist's picture of hope, triumphant over the world's sin and sorrow, triumphant over anything and everything that can hurt a human being. When all else is gone, one still has hope and hope can triumph.

There are many stories of people who were inspired by Watts' painting. One that I like tells of a man who was on his way to drown himself. On the way he saw this painting in a store window. He looked carefully at the blindfolded woman on her world of misery, playing on the one string. Finally, he said, "Well, I have one string – I have a little boy at home," and he retraced his steps.

In one form or another, that story can be repeated countless times. No matter how bad life is, if you will only look, you can always find one hope that is left and that one hope can be the saving power.

I have before me a letter from a friend telling me of a marvelous change that has come into his life, the birth of his son. He says, "I have something else to think about, and a new hope." Certainly it is true that "life is full of glad surprises for those who hope."

The Tide Will Come In

The ocean fascinates me. One spring in Puerta Vallarta, Mexico my wife and I went to sleep each night for a week to the melody of the breakers coming in upon the shore. We ate breakfast every morning looking out across the vastness of the water. We walked several miles down the beach. We swam out into the deep and then rode the waves back in. As we lived by the ocean for that time, there came a better understanding of life because the two are so much alike. Life itself has a vastness that is beyond the reach of our sight.

There are many parallels between life and the ocean, but one especially impresses me – the coming and going of the tides. The tide goes out and the water level becomes very low; the tide comes in and the water level is high again. There is no power on earth that can prevent the movement of the tides. So it is with an individual life – we experience times of personal low tide and of high tide and there is no way to stop these movements. If we realize that we will experience low tides of our spirit, then our moments of depression and discouragement lose much of their terror.

Many times as a counselor I have had phone calls from a frantic person saying, "I must see you today. I just cannot go on." But often circumstances were such that I could not see the person that day. Several days later when I had time, I would telephone and the person would say, "I feel better now. I'll be all right." What happened? The tide had come in.

Sometimes the burdens of sorrow are so heavy we cannot bear them. But sorrow is a natural part of the experience of living. In the midst of this low-tide of life, we need to learn to wait for the high tide to return. Our agony is not permanent. Though it may feel like a dark night is settling down on you, the morning will come. So we carry on through our sorrow, knowing it will bring us to the brightness of a new day.

I was in New York City a few years ago and saw one of the giant ships of the ocean coming in. It was beautiful and powerful and proud looking. But majestic as it was, that great ship had to wait for the tide before it could come in. The captain was anxious to make port. There were passengers on board who were in a hurry to land. But no matter – they must wait for the tide.

There are times when we are anxious to make some port of success, to accomplish some task; these are times when we must wait for the tide. In the waiting, we are certain the tide will rise, and because of that certainty we have faith and hope.

Principles To Live By

As I look back over the years, I can discern principles that have been dominant in my thinking. I feel that these principles have pretty much shaped my life. I'm sure that if you think about it, you too have your own set of principles which have made you the person you are.

1. **Believing in People** - The first principle is, "I believe in people." My belief in people has come mainly, as a result of people's belief in me. I have never felt it was my duty to fuss at people or criticize them. I have never felt that it was necessary to preach about their faults. Most people know about their weaknesses. I felt it was my job to let people know that I was concerned about them and loved them, believed in them, and wanted to help them. This has been a controlling principle of my life.

2. **Living Affirmatively** - I feel as if, for the most part, I have lived affirmatively. I have tried to concentrate on possibilities instead of problems. I believe it is better to emphasize triumphs than troubles. There is more power in emphasizing our faith than our fears. Once I was driving along and the traffic was stopped. On the side of the road I saw some men sinking some large steel beams into the ground. I asked one of the men what he was doing. He explained to me that the ground under the road was shifting. They were sinking some of the beams to give stability to the roadbed. I have felt that it was of great value to sink into one's mind some great truths. Suppose one really comes to understand and accept this

truth: "I love myself as I am today." Just that one statement can tremendously affect a life.

3. **Having the Power of Faith** – Increasingly through the years I have believed that no person is ever defeated until he or she thinks so. We have tremendous powers if we use them. There are five laws of faith:

First, you have faith.

Second, always start with your faith instead of your fears.

Third, no matter what happens, hold on to your faith.

Fourth, do not be afraid to trust your heart.

Fifth, maintain a spirit of humility

I believe that we all have unused powers which if properly motivated, can accomplish things we never dreamed we could.

4. **Knowing Your Deepest Desire** – I've often heard it said, "Be careful what you set your heart on, for you will surely get it." I think the trouble with a lot of people is they never know what they want. Across the years, I have used a six-part formula that has really worked for me. Let me share it with you:

First, decide what you really want.

Second, write down on paper this dominant desire of yours.

Third, after you have stated this idea in not more than fifty words, then memorize it and several times each day repeat it aloud.

Fourth, test your idea.

Fifth, after clarifying your thinking, and thoroughly testing your motives and purposes, then you are ready for the main event – begin to pray.

Sixth, do all you can to accomplish your own desire.

5. **Taking Time and Letting Go** – A long time ago I decided that probably the worst sin of my own life was being in too big a hurry. I made some changes and for many years now I have slowed down. I have twenty-four hours every day. Nobody has any more hours than I have, and I decided that I would spend some of my time on me. I am a bit like a friend of mine who once said to me, "I have never been happier since I resigned as General Manager of the Universe." I long ago learned that I do not have to do everything. What I'm trying to say is that I have decided that I do not have to run through life. I am just not in as big a hurry as I used to think I had to be, and the amazing thing is I feel like I accomplish a lot more now than I used to! There is a little phrase that has been in my mind for years. It goes like this: "The hurrieder I go, the behinder I get." Another great phrase is, "Those who cannot let go – cannot hang on."

Look Forward Hopefully

This request came in the mail after one of my articles appeared in *Today's Woman*: "Please tell me how to gain confidence in tomorrow and to face the future with calmness." This letter went on to say, "I realize there isn't much I can do about the past; I can work with the present, but when I think of all that might happen in the future, I feel helpless and afraid."

The first step toward a calm confidence in the future is to learn to believe that life is good. That principle applies to the future equally as it does to the present or to the past. That doesn't mean that everything that happens will be good. Life is composed of joy and sorrow, victory and defeat, success and failure. We know that tomorrow will probably bring both good and bad into our lives. Knowing that, we must think of life as a whole instead of merely separate and independent experiences.

Here is an illustration: think of a ship. The purpose of a ship is to sail across the seas – but not all parts of a ship will float. The engine, for example, if put in the water would immediately sink. So would the propeller, the compass and many other pieces of the ship. But when all of the parts of the ship are securely built together, it does sail.

So it is with life. Some things will happen to us that are bad. Some things will be good. But when we consider all the experiences of life, then life as a whole will work out for the good. That is the faith we really want. We do not ask for the assurance that all the sorrows, disappointments and troubles be eliminated from our tomorrows. We don't really want that.

There is a Greek legend about a woman who came to the River Styx to be carried across to the next life. Charon, the man who ran the ferry, reminded her that she could drink of the waters of Lethe and thus forget the life she was leaving. Eagerly she said, "I will forget how I have suffered." But he pointed out, "You will forget how you have rejoiced." "I will forget my failures," she said. "And you will forget your victories," he added. "I will forget how I have been hated," she said. "And also how you have been loved," he added. The story ends with the woman deciding it was better to retain her memory of the bad in order to also retain her memory of the good.

So it is with the future. If by drinking some magic water we could eliminate the suffering, failure and hate of tomorrow, we would eagerly do it. But we must remember that life is always two-sided and to destroy one side by necessity destroys the other. Therefore, we would also eliminate the joy, victory and love. We would not drink the magic water.

Some things that happen in life are bad. Some things that happen are good. But life itself can be trusted. When we have faith, we face tomorrow with hope instead of fear. Why do we worry about tomorrow? Not because we're afraid something bad might happen. We know there are sorrows and defeats ahead for us. You can stand anything, even the deepest pain, if you know, really know, you will get through it.

With faith, our fears of tomorrow give way to hope and when we look forward with hope, life is good. One of the purest gems of all literature is Tennyson's "In Memoriam." In it you find this wonderful line, "The mighty hopes that make us men." Hope gives strength to life.

There was a study done of a large group of people who worked together in an office. They all did about the same work, yet, at the end of the day, some were limp with fatigue while others seemed strong and rested. It was discovered that the energetic group had something to look forward to –

a party that night, a weekend trip, something pleasant do to at home – while the other tired group had nothing to look forward to. If you want to develop genuine hope, you must have something definite to hope for. Hope is never real until it has an object. I have suggested two questions to many people: (1) What is something you really desire in life? (2) How can you get started toward that goal? Those two questions lead to the transformation of a goal into creative action. When we have that, we automatically eliminate most of our fears. We just don't have time to worry.

Once a new highway was being built in England. It was to run between Holborn and the Strand. In the way stood a very, very old building. The workmen tore the building down and cleared the ground on which it stood. After the ground had been exposed to the sunshine and rain for some months, a wonderful thing happened. Flowers began to spring up, and botanists and naturalists from all over England came to study them. Many of the flowers were identified as being a species the Romans had brought to England almost 2,000 years before. Some of the plants that sprang up are completely unknown today. Hidden there in the ground, without air or light, the seeds seemed to have died. But they were not dead. As soon as the obstacles were cleared away, and the sunshine let in, they burst forth into the fullness of their beauty.

So the seeds of eternal life are in every human life. Often those seeds are buried under such things as disbelief, selfishness, pride, lust, preoccupation, or other obstacles. There is a wonderful life within reach of every person – our promised land. The rainbow means the storm has past. It is a symbol calling us to look forward hopefully.